Trees

Trees

For Shelter and Shade,
For Memory and Magic

Charles Fenyvesi

St. Martin's Press New York

TREES: FOR SHELTER AND SHADE, FOR MEMORY AND MAGIC. Copyright © 1992
by Charles Fenyvesi. All rights reserved. Printed in the United States
of America. No part of this book may be used or reproduced in any
manner whatsoever without written permission except in the case of
brief quotations embodied in critical articles or reviews. For
information, address St. Martin's Press, 175 Fifth Avenue, New York,
N.Y. 10010.

Production Editor: David Stanford Burr

Design by Jaye Zimet

Library of Congress Cataloging-in-Publication Data

Fenyvesi, Charles.
        Trees : for shelter and shade, for memory and magic /
Charles Fenyvesi.
                p. cm.
        "A Thomas Dunne book."
        ISBN 0-312-07102-7
        1. Arboriculture. 2. Trees. 3. Shade trees. I. Title.
SB435.F46   1992
634.9—dc20   91-36497
                                                           CIP

First Edition: March 1992

10 9 8 7 6 5 4 3 2 1

ACKNOWLEDGMENT

Giving thanks

  I am beholden to many individuals, only some of whom are mentioned by name in the following pages, who inspired and educated me on the subject of our faithful friends, the trees. I also want to express my thanks to *The Washington Post's* Home Section, where in my weekly column, *The Ornamental Gardener,* many of the paragraphs printed in this book were first published, albeit in a different form. I am grateful to my literary agent, Joseph Spieler, who patiently and thoughtfully waited for years until this book germinated, took root, and sprouted some foliage, and to my editor, Tom Dunne, whose enthusiasm for the project was a source of inspiration to me.

Contents

Creator of All Good Things . . .
We thank you
        for the beauty of the plant,
        for the strength of its healing,
        for the goodness of its color,
        for the strength of its smell,
        and the cleanness of its spirit.

—from "Song of the Seven Herbs," by
        Walking Night Bear

Trees

Basics

"When a man plants a tree, he plants himself."

—John Muir

1
Why a Tree?

In every yard there is a certain spot that is waiting for a tree. But not for just any tree. That tree should be the right one for the person who plants it.

⚘ A Norway maple is a solidly practical choice for the energetic young man or woman who wants a stately tree with lots of foliage and plenty of shade—and as much of both as possible, and as soon as possible. In contrast, the slow-growing walnut tree is for the patient parent who thinks generations ahead: a dozen years may have to pass before the harvest fills a bushel basket, and even then the branches may not be sturdy enough for climbing for several more years, perhaps until a grandchild comes along. A Kwanzan cherry tree with limbs like a Javanese dancer's is for the sensitive soul drawn to such Oriental mysticism as breaking winter's spell with a blizzard of petals. And for the traditionalist whose desire is for a straight-trunked, majestic tree that can make the human heart quiver, the white oak is the one.

⚘ The personality of a tree echoes the mind of its beholder. For some people, the weeping willow is lugubrious; for others, its yards-long, pendulous branches cascading from a robust trunk form a gazebo and offer the advantage of being able to observe the outside world without being observed by it. A clump of paper birches, their bark white with black markings, stands for the puritan simplicity of New England woods, or, for Europeans, the deep melancholy of the Slavic heartland. For one admirer, the symmetrical, pyramid-shaped Colorado spruce is a case of natural perfection; for another, beauty is defined by the twisted, ragged frame of a Monterey pine: a tormented tree defying storm and salt spray, and subsisting on whatever dirt and debris have settled on its rocky ledge. To some gardeners, sitting in the scented shade of a linden tree in July or taking a September stroll through an allée of horse chestnut trees strewn with spiny burrs is singularly conducive to meditation. Others associate such spaces with relaxation or romance.

&❧ However, some functions are universal. In the heat of the summer, a shade tree is a luxury that we can hardly do without. The shade cast by trees is never sunless darkness, but modulated, filtered sunlight. Nor does a screen of trees form a spite fence, cutting off neighbors. A living fence is a most friendly form of separation: while setting boundaries, it allows conversation and peeks across.

&❧ For millennia, trees have been singled out as objects of worship and tools of magic. The spiral wand the Druids used for divination had to be ash, admired as a "tree of life," and only an ash stake driven through a corpse immobilized a ghost in Bronze Age Ireland. The sacred fires of ancient Rome were always made with oak, the tree identified with Jupiter—also with the Germanic Thor and the Hellenic Zeus—along with the thunderbolt that the chief of the gods targeted on the tallest of tall oaks. To drive out evil spirits, pious Jews commemorating the Feast of Tabernacles still beat the walls of their houses and synagogues with bundles of willow branches.

&❧ The first places that people called gardens were groves of trees that no human hand had planted or tended yet were so beautiful that the locals believed they must have emanated from a supernatural being. In Celtic languages, trees are also letters—or perhaps it was originally the other way around. The alphabet known as Beth-Luis-Nion, which translates into English as birch-rowan-ash, takes its name from a sequence of trees held sacred by the Druids and whose initials are its letters. As described by Robert Graves, the English poet who lived what he called the best years of his life in a mountain village on the Mediterranean island of Majorca, that alphabet "consists of five vowels and thirteen consonants, each letter corresponding to the tree which it honors. The thirteen consonants correspond to the lunar months of the year, while the five tree-vowels mark the stations of the sun through the seasons. Together they form the lunar calendar of seasonal tree-magic." In his book *The White Goddess,* Graves declares that the language of poetic myth "anciently current in the Mediterranean and Northern Europe was a magical language bound up with popular religious ceremonies in honor of the Moon-goddess, or Muse, some of them dating from the Old Stone Age, and that this remains the language of true poetry—'true' in the nostalgic modern sense of 'the unimprovable original, not a synthetic substitute.'"

&. Nowadays many of our most thoughtful scientists are convinced that trees offer the best way to cope with pollution and other environmental stresses, and that the various negative developments summed up in the phrase "global warming" can be best fought on the home ground, and particularly in our cities, by planting more and more trees. The American Forestry Association (AFA) has called for planting one hundred million trees in our towns and cities to reverse the effects of destroyed tropical forests and increased burning of fossil fuel. "Laboratory models show that having three shade trees on the south and west sides of a house can lower air-conditioning bills by up to a half," writes Neil Sampson, head of the AFA. "The total effect, in terms of reduced power demands and energy consumption, could translate into a significant impact on national carbon dioxide reduction goals." While Ronald Reagan ridiculed "tree huggers," spoke of "killer trees," and refused to force industry to clean up its act, his successor, George Bush, seems to be friendly to trees and has endorsed the AFA's program, called Global ReLeaf.

☙ Alden Townsend, a U.S. Department of Agriculture research specialist, claims that we can improve the environment by choosing only the hardiest and most disease-free trees, and by avoiding what is known and criticized as monoculture—the repetition of a handful of popular species already gracing other gardens in the neighborhood.

☙ Marc Cathey, former director of the National Arboretum, has called for "a new gardening ethic," urging every American to plant as many trees as possible in the home garden and in the community. He recommends native and meticulously developed "superplants" that can flourish without chemical intervention and have proved that they are well adapted to the climate of each of the eleven zones based on coldest day of the year temperature, of the United States.

☙ Once a tree is selected and planted—for whatever reason—it doesn't take long to develop an affinity with it. The asymmetry of an unusual spruce has become the logo of a nonconformist Washington attorney I know. Standing by the gate of his estate, his spruce says: I do it my way. For another tree lover, the graceful ovals of his twin Japanese persimmon trees, which ornament his front yard, and the bumper crops of the sweet-and-tart fruit they yield year after year offer a message of classical beauty and biblical abundance. Harvesting the persimmons, the size of an orange, and giving them to friends has become a high point of his life.

☙ A garden is both the most public and the most private living space. While a rationalist may insist on planting varieties recommended for the region by the most reputable experts, a romantic will strive to create a garden where metaphors are concrete and the tangible is illusory. A great garden is seldom created in a year or two but happens over a long span of time, in an ideal world, the work of several generations may be incorporated. But the outcome of the tug-of-war between nature's will and its tenants' whim is never more than a halftime score.

• Much of gardening is based on affection—instincts we are born with and have a chance to refine, and the affinities we develop in that process. The more we garden, the better we get at knowing what nature wants us to do. On the other hand, the more we discover what we really like and how to make that special plant of preference prosper, the more that plant will prosper—which in turn will only enhance our affection for it.

• It is a good idea to have a favorite tree, just as it is a good idea to have a favorite season and a favorite poet. Every spring I look forward to seeing my pear trees burst into bloom, and they never disappoint, just as I may read William Wordsworth again and again, and come upon something new, rather than run into a boring sameness.

• In an ideal world, the person who plants a tree remains to enjoy watching the sapling shoot upward and spread into a stately tree. But even if such stability is seldom a realistic prospect in our society of frequent movers, the tree will stay there as a memento more enduring than any finished basement or extra bathroom one might have added to the property. As one drives by the old homestead, it is a thrill—and sometimes a bit of a heartache—to see what has become of the little sapling one planted long, long ago.

• Annual flowers live for one year and then scatter their seeds; perennial flowers die to the ground in the winter and then come up from their roots in the spring. But the life of a tree is closer to the human scale. Protected by their bark, trunk and branches go dormant as the first killing frost approaches, and although some trees live for centuries, many others, for instance most fruit trees, die after fifty, sixty, or seventy years.

• Trees are our constant companions, signposts on roads and landmarks on open fields. Most of us feel that something is amiss in a treeless landscape, which we are inclined to call lunar to distance it from the earth and ourselves. We know without consulting our encyclopedias—for these are the kind of facts we feel in our guts—that trees have existed for many millions of years and are the largest life forms ever to inhabit this planet.

&❦ American Indians think of trees as our elders: trees were here before a child was born; they are likely to be here after that child dies, even if that child lives to the fullness of his or her days. Regardless of the tribe, Indian religious ceremonies make use of cedar, a tree they worship, and whenever possible, they like to hold their powwows under the limbs of great live oaks, such as the one in the eighteenth-century plantation Middleton Place near Charleston, South Carolina. That monumental tree has a horizontal spread of 145 feet and a height of 85 feet. It is at least a thousand years old and still growing, visited by hundreds of tourists every day. But, alas, no more Indians meet in its shade.

&❦ The inheritance of a grand old tree is a treasure to be cherished. One homeowner I know is lucky enough to have in his backyard a magnificent tulip poplar, thought to be more than two hundred years old, thus predating the American Revolution. One of the first things he did after buying the property was to install powerful spotlights to illuminate the tree. Off and on, he has also talked about upgrading his lawn or perhaps putting in a flower garden, but over the years he has done nothing. He has concluded that he needs no garden: his guests admire the tree, the largest in the neighborhood, and he expects them to pay no attention to the surrounding grass, which is scraggly, or the bushes, which are neglected.

&❦ In traditional societies around the world, people act upon the feelings they have about trees. In pagan New Guinea and modern England, in Jewish culture and in the Protestant Midwest, the birth of a child and the death of a beloved relative, a move into a new house and the start of a business venture are the kinds of event that call for planting a tree—a tree of memory. To reflect—or to deflect—a family catharsis, few activities are as positively commemorative as the launching of a tree.

❧ Though some gardeners are in the habit of adding a blessing after the small mound around the tree trunk is carefully tamped down, verbal piety is not a requisite. But it is a good idea to let the family witness the planting and assist it. And let the tree be known and remembered for the event that occasioned its planting.

2
Whens and Hows of Planting

T he ideal time to plant a tree is on a chilly, unpleasant, overcast day in the fall. It looks like rain at any moment, and heavy clouds and the likelihood of scattered thundershowers are forecast for the week ahead.

🍃 For people who plan an outdoor wedding, such prospects are dismal. But no circumstances are more promising for the launching of a tree that we hope will be with us for years to come.

🍃 If the sapling comes from a mail-order firm, it is best to dig the hole first and then undo the layers of paper and plastic that keep the plant from drying out. When buying in a nursery, we should spend time picking the sturdiest specimen, the one that looks most promising.

🍃 Container-grown trees are a bit more expensive than those sold with their roots bare. While the ball of earth around the roots helps to ensure survival in the new site and reduces to a minimum any transplant shock, the risks are not much greater with bare roots. What matters is that close contact is established between the roots and the soil at the time of planting, to be followed by a generous dose of water every day for three days, or longer if the weather turns sunny and warm.

🍃 When transporting a bare-root tree in a car, take special

care not to let the wind dry out the roots. Putting the tree in the back of the station wagon and allowing the roots to stick out could dehydrate the plant to the point that it dies, even if the roots are wrapped in burlap.

🍃 A sapling grown in a container or balled-and-burlapped (B&B) should be soaked before it is placed in the ground. With a bare-root plant, prudence calls for keeping it in a bucket of water for an hour or so prior to planting.

🍃 There is some evidence that bare-root trees are healthier than the ones sold in a container or balled-and-burlapped because they do not carry with them diseases and bacteria from their original sites. They respond quickly and positively—by growing fast—to their new environment, particularly if the soil they are set in is porous and rich.

🍃 Throughout the fall, trees and shrubs are usually sold at a discount. The plant business is winding down and managers try to reduce the number of specimens they have to take care of during the winter.

🍃 When planting, it is critical to spread the roots out evenly and far, and in every direction. Do not wind the roots in a circle around the hole because they may eventually strangle the trunk. Prune back any injured roots.

🍃 If an assistant is available, he or she should hold the tree as the soil is backfilled into the hole and tamped down once in a while to ensure good contact between the roots and the soil. Keeping the tree straight while the hole is filled is an educational experience for a child, who can be reminded years later about their relative heights at the time of planting and their growth spurts since. If no assistant is available, the tines of a spading fork laid down on the ground can hold the tree upright.

🍃 Some experts recommend cutting back the branches by about a third to balance the roots that are usually lost in transplanting. There is also a dissenting opinion, in fact, the latest trend, calling such cutbacks unnecessary—which is yet another proof that gardening is a craft practiced by individuals rather than a science seeking consensus. However, there is agreement on the need to remove injured and puny branches with a pair of sharp shears.

🐚 Experts shape a little basin around the leader to catch water. Wrapping the leader (main trunk) with special paper sold in garden centers will prevent winter damage and discourage gnawing by squirrels and field mice, deer and rabbits. Staking with one or more sturdy two-by-twos six-foot-high (preferably oak because it will hold up for several years) is a good idea, particularly if the winds are strong and the tree came bare-root, and fastening is safest with strong wire threaded through a piece of garden hose to protect the bark. (Here is a great opportunity to utilize that punctured garden hose you have been reluctant to toss into the trash.)

🐚 For fruit trees and their ornamental varieties that bear only insignificant fruit, the planting site should be at a high rather than low point of the topography. Cold air flows into low pockets and collects there, causing frost injury in late fall and early spring when fruit trees such as peaches and cherries bud and flower.

🐚 Location is critical. In the case of most trees, there must be a distance of at least twenty feet between the tree and the house—and thirty is even better. If the tree is closer, roots in search of moisture and nourishment may probe the weaknesses of a cinder-block foundation or a concrete patio, and the odds are better than even that both the tree and the structure will suffer as a result. Just as roots of street trees often push up and split the pavement, they can damage the walls and the floors of a house. Some trees, such as poplars and silver maples, keep sending out roots to seek out sewers and other sources of water and eventually may crack and crush concrete to get to the source of additional moisture. If unsuccessful, the tree's root system may be blocked and stunted.

🐚 The distance between trees should be carefully studied, and the location of planting sites must be determined by the eventual height and root spread of the trees, not on the basis of their current dimensions. It is amazing how people who make plans for the high school their toddlers may attend will buy a three-foot-high pagoda tree and expect it to grow only a few more feet, even though a mature tree is known to reach a height of forty feet.

• There ought to be a warning sticker on every sapling. For instance: "In twenty years, this red maple may reach a height of sixty feet, and its branches will spread twenty-five feet from the trunk. DO NOT PLANT IT CLOSE TO THE HOUSE!"

• Give the tree enough space. If it is a case of tight quarters, a dwarf variety may be the solution. Requiring an area of only about ten by ten feet and growing no taller than twelve feet, a dwarf cherry or apple can nevertheless provide standard-size fruit. For the confined spaces of townhouse lots, Japanese maples and Alberta spruce perform admirably.

• For trees of all types, fertile soil with good drainage is the ideal growth medium. It is important to avoid planting trees in those spots where water will stand in a puddle for an hour after a substantial rain. But there are exceptions such as the weeping willow and river birch, which thrive on moisture that other trees would consider excessive.

• If the soil is compacted and puddles are evident after every rainfall, dig up the area and mix in a lot of sand or organic matter such as compost, rotted leaves, or aged horse manure. Or perhaps a drain line is needed.

• Make sure that grasses and weeds do not grow in the area above the roots of a tree just planted. Trees do not like competition for moisture and nourishment. Particularly when they are young, their development may be substantially set back by just a few clumps of grassplants or weeds. Some trees, such as walnuts, exude a poisonous substance to retard the growth of grass; other trees simply produce dense shade to discourage competition.

• A two-inch-thick layer of pine bark or hardwood mulch is one fine alternative to a green ground cover. Another esthetically pleasing solution that is good for the tree is a circle of pebbles or river rocks around the trunk.

❧ The size of the planting hole is a matter of intense controversy. For decades, guidelines called for digging a hole at least twice as deep and wide as the rootball. A different formula came from seasoned gardeners who suggested a hole twice the size of that recommended on the nursery's instruction label. As for the space between the rootball—or roots—and the undisturbed ground, it was to be backfilled with bags of choice topsoil or compost mixed in, about half and half, with some of the original soil from the hole.

❧ In recent years, expert opinion has been shifting in favor of a hole that is wide rather than deep. For instance, the International Society of Arboriculture now calls for "a satellite-dish hole," and declares that "twice the width of the rootball is good, three times is even better."

❧ "Roots need to grow beyond the edges of the original planting hole into the surrounding soil if a tree is to survive more than a few years after planting," Thomas Perry declared recently in the newsletter "Urban Forest Forum." Perry's argument radically revises conventional wisdom: he recommends that the soil be prepared in the entire area that will eventually support the tree. Thus, if one expects that a three-inch-diameter sapling will grow into a vigorous ten-inch-diameter tree, the soil should be prepared in a circle with a radius of twenty feet.

❧ Preparation means breaking up the soil to a depth of ten inches, Perry writes, because roughly ninety percent of the roots will be in that worked-over and improved upper layer of the soil. As for the planting hole, Perry believes that it is sufficient to dig the size recommended by the nursery, and, moreover, contrary to conventional wisdom, the bottom of the rootball should rest on undisturbed soil.

❧ Neil Sampson, head of the American Forestry Association, offers yet another theory. He suggests digging far, far deeper. Working in northern Virginia he has gone down as deep as four feet in order to reach underneath the so-called blue clay, which virtually impervious to water. He keeps digging until he reaches a level that allows one inch of water to drain in one hour.

&. Using this method, Sampson has planted a sycamore sapling in August, which is one of the worst times to plant a tree because of the heat. (His excuse is that he was given the tree as a present and he had no choice but to plant it right away.) Nevertheless, the sycamore grew a spectacular twenty-two inches before dormancy set in three months later.

&. To soften the impact of the August heat, Sampson soaked the planting area, a circle with a radius of four feet, and the backfill he used was an exceptionally rich mix of compost and leaf mold.

&. Both Perry and Sampson advance their arguments to counter the sad facts of urban planting: typical trees in city parks have a life expectancy of twenty-five to thirty years; trees along suburban streets may survive up to eighteen years; and downtown trees in planting holes squeezed in between the asphalt of the street and the sidewalk often have to be replaced in three to four years. Clearly, the smaller the planting area that is prepared, the shorter will be the life of the tree.

&. Perry uses the example of the bonsai, a tree kept on purpose in a shallow container so it becomes a dwarf. He compares a city tree to a bonsai plant that needs to be dug up, its roots pruned, and its depleted soil replaced every year or so. "We are presently unable to design small planting sites that do not require comparable care," he concludes. A tree will not fulfill its height potential if its roots do not have the freedom to spread. One sign of the tree roots' thwarted search for expansion is "girdling": roots grow in circles in the backfill of the planting hole because they cannot break through the compacted—and sometimes stony—soil beyond the planting hole. Sooner or later, girdling chokes the tree because the roots cannot breathe.

&. Digging a large hole, providing top-quality soil for the backfill, and working over the ground in the surrounding area do not seem to be an exorbitant price to pay if one considers that a tree is a lifetime investment. Experts say shade trees can reduce cooling costs by as much as twenty percent and their foliage contributes to the reduction of the carbon dioxide buildup.

❧ In the Talmud, the voluminous Jewish compilation of laws and legends, it is written that if a person engaged in the process of planting a tree hears someone shouting that the Messiah has arrived, he should first complete the job at hand. Only after the tree is properly placed in its hole, the soil is tamped down, and the planting area is soaked may the planter of the tree proceed to leave the site and see for himself if the Messiah has indeed come.

3
The Season of the Root

Fall is the prime season of the root. Hidden deep in the ground like buried treasure, the network of roots is the least-known part of the tree. Nevertheless, the root is a critical factor, and for people engaged in the enterprise of horticulture or agriculture, the root's cycle of growth is as fraught with significance as the phases of the moon.

❧ A tree has one schedule for its assets above the ground and another for what lies beneath. Branches, leaves, and flowers do virtually all their sprouting and growing in the spring and the summer—at a time when root growth is minimal. On the other hand, studies have shown that more than eighty percent of all root development takes place during the fall—at a time when the plant's above-ground parts are at their most passive, gradually withdrawing into dormancy. In fact, roots keep on expanding even after the rest of the plant has gone dormant—right up to the time when the ground freezes over.

❧ One reason for this sudden, intense activity during the fall is that the root is the one part of the plant that prefers temperatures in the sixties and will still thrive when the thermostat dips as low as the fifties. Even when air temperature drops to the low forties and upper thirties—which is discouragingly chilly for every other part of the plant—the roots, insulated by the soil, keep absorbing nutrients and moisture, and they thicken and spread. Soil temperature can still be in the low forties when a frost nips the top of the plant.

❧ When establishing a tree—or a shrub or a bulbous perennial—nothing is as important as making sure it has a chance to develop a solid foundation: a healthy, extensive root system. Once the plant gets going in the spring and begins to manufacture its food, the shoots and the leaves will start channeling nutrients to the roots, which serve as a storehouse. The longer and more numerous the roots are, the more food they can store. In addition, roots also draw nutrients from the soil, and the deeper and wider they reach, the more nutrients they will collect.

❧ The difference in the peak periods of the different parts of the tree also explains a puzzle: in climates where winter brings freezing temperatures, fertilizing trees and shrubs is not recommended after midsummer, but considered useful after the plant has entered its dormancy. The fact is that post-midsummer fertilizing encourages plenty of tender new growth that will not have the time to acquire winter-hardiness and will probably die back after the first hard freeze. But if the fertilizer is applied after the leaves have fallen and the top of the plant has stopped growing, the roots will still be able to benefit.

❧ On account of the peak root activity, fall is the best time to plant most trees and shrubs (known as *woody perennials,* because their woody stems survive winter) as well as many flowers (known as *herbaceous perennials,* because they die down to the ground in the winter). While a healthy tree may be planted at any time during the growing season—with the high heat of summer being the most risky—prudence suggests midway between the heat of summer and the first frost.

❧ There is, however, a sophisticated argument for spring planting of bare-root trees. It is based on the observation that when a tree is dug up bare-rooted and later replanted, it loses in that process a large percentage—probably the great majority—of its root surface. No question about it, most of the root tips and the rootlets, as well as the hairlike roots, are lost when the plant is shaken loose from its original soil environment. Thus the plant will be busy trying to grow back what it just lost, the argument concludes, and not be able to devote much energy to the critical job of absorbing moisture and nutrients.

 ❧ Without a doubt, digging up a plant, shaking off its soil, and then replanting it amounts to a sudden and traumatic change, from which many plants need time to recover. However, some plants seem to thrive on such trauma. For instance, walnut saplings have growth spurts after they are dug up and then replanted bare-rooted. They appear to love the move and enjoy exploring their new environment.

 ❧ Spring is the second-best season to plant a tree. For many people, "it feels just right" to launch trees at a time when every plant under the sun "seems to take off."

 ❧ The root is the part of the plant we understand the least. Virgil says that the oak's roots extend as deep in the ground as its branches rise in the air. But even nowadays we have only estimates of how far and how deep the roots of a particular tree go. Similarly, we have only a limited knowledge of the bacteria and pests that live off the roots—and how they affect the life and death of a tree. What we do know is that roots anchor a plant best when they have a large area of improved, porous soil to penetrate.

 ❧ Unlike leaves that often curl up, roots do not have a way to signal that they need water. But we do know that tree roots appreciate a thorough soak or two if the summer or the fall is dry and even after the above-the-ground parts have gone into dormancy. Watering before the first hard freeze is expected is especially helpful. The result is a stronger plant that will get through winter unscathed, and better prepared for its growth spurt in the spring.

4
Standing Alone, Standing Proud

Ιf your soul or your landscape—shouldn't one reflect the other?—cries out for the drama of a solitary, singularly expressive plant, or if you have space for but one tree, the decision-making process should begin with considerations of size and shape.

ɶ Trees in oval and globe shapes offer a well-tailored, formal elegance, even a touch of Versailles. In this category, trees worth considering include dozens of varieties of red maples and crab apples, ash and hawthorn, globe locust and Chinese scholar tree. To choose one from among them, it is best to visit your area's largest and best-stocked tree nursery, and ask to be shown trees in the shape and eventual size desired.

ɶ As in a clothing store, the variety is overwhelming, and you have to know your own mind. It helps if you have already narrowed down the selection to a few species, on the basis of trees pictured in garden books and catalogs or observed in parks or other people's yards. But it is also possible to make a good choice by identifying the tree you find most simpatico through intensive browsing in a nursery. For a comprehensive survey, it is best to visit an arboretum, which not only displays the finest specimens with labels identifying botanical name andindividual variety, but gives an opportunity to size up trees as they look in their mature, even venerable phase.

&▲ Your interest in and preference for a particular fall color are important, as the difference in the hue is often what sets apart one variety from another. For instance, the red maple called October Glory turns crimson and keeps its leaves until Thanksgiving—long after other red maples have dropped theirs—while another maple, called Green Mountain Sugar Maple, offers shades of orange and scarlet.

&▲ Vase-shaped trees—which in fact look more like ice cream cones—are a little less formal than oval- and globe-shaped varieties, and they provide better shade. White and red oaks, tulip trees and sweet gums form some of the finest vases. An outstanding selection in this category is Zelkova Green Vase, which looks like the American elm, once the premier street tree but now vanishing because of its proneness to disease. Zelkova Green Vase is exceptionally hardy and disease resistant, and it is a fast grower, adding as much as three feet of growth per year to a possible height of eighty feet. Another variety of Zelkova that looks like the American elm and is often planted as a substitute is the Village Green Zelkova. It is a vigorous grower, straight trunked with arching branches, and a favorite with city planners because of its tolerance of pollution and poor soil.

&▲ The sycamore, also known as the plane tree, is roughly vase-shaped as well, but is better described as "gaunt." Bent, twisted, and vigorously asymmetrical, sycamores tower over three-story houses. At ground level, the trunk can easily reach four feet across and, much like whipped cream over a cup of hot chocolate, it has a habit of spilling, over several square feet of the ground. But the most dramatic part of a sycamore is its peeling bark, flaking off in irregular patches rounded at the edges, most of them about the size of the human hand. The outermost skin is cinnamon brown; then come layers of several shades of gray, including slate gray and Prussian gray; then light brown turning cream, along with undertones of a surprising salmon pink. The deepest layer is a luminous, almost chalky white, which makes an old sycamore with fully exfoliated bark look ghostly, particularly on a dark night and with the wind making the branches tremble and groan.

❧ But there is nothing ghostlike about an old ornamental cherry tree of a similarly random branch structure, which keeps producing blizzards of white or pink flowers for up to two weeks each spring. The tree's oldest part, the lower section of the trunk, looks like a silky fabric that has partially unraveled, and its once rich reddish-burgundy coloring has faded into a dusky gray with just a suggestion of ruby. During winter, the color is an earthy brown, but summer brings back a glimmer of red.

❧ On the other hand, a pyramid-shaped tree has that precise symmetry that many homeowners look for. In this category, lindens, European ashes, and magnolias are among the most popular.

❧ Standing by itself, a tree shaped like a column looks like an exclamation point. The consensus among landscape designers and gardeners is that such a tree—for instance, juniper, the white birch Fastigiata, and mountain ash—looks better when there are several of them, in a row or a clump. Virtually all the major tree species have columnar varieties.

❧ While such trees are carefully selected and hybridized forms, each designed for a sturdy, disciplined, upright (some would call it uptight) framework as the breeding objective, pendulous or "weeping" trees come about because branches turn out to be devoid of the chemical that would stiffen them and render them upright. Thus the quality of hanging limp, however esthetically intriguing it may seem, is in fact a deficiency.

❧ A pendulous tree strikes most people as having a sorrowful, haunting, melancholy appearance. In Celtic mythology, the willow—unquestionably the best-known pendulous tree, even the pendulous tree par excellence—symbolizes the death aspects of the moon goddess, and it was worshiped by witches. In Greece, the willow was sacred to Hera, Circe, and Persephone—all enchantresses leading men to death. According to Robert Graves, the words "witch" and "wicked" are derived from the same ancient word for willow, which is also responsible for "wicker." The poet says that under the full moon, the druidical human sacrifices were offered in wicker baskets and that funerary flints were chipped in the shape of a willow leaf.

❧ The association of willow and sorrow was strengthened by the Bible, which describes Jews who had been forcibly taken from their homeland crying by the river Babylon some 2,600 years ago, remembering Jerusalem and hanging their lyres on the willows flanking the river.

❧ In an article in the *Journal of Arboriculture,* Frank Santamour and Alice McArdle, both of the National Arboretum, argue that those willows cited in Psalm 137 were in fact poplars and that the weeping willow, *Salix babylonica* in botanical Latin, is probably native to China. They go on to say that the weeping willows cultivated in the United States are not *Salix babylonica,* as it is popularly believed, and furthermore, that their host of variety names—from Annularis to Wisconsin through Matsudana, Niobe, and Sepulcralis—are incorrect and confusing, and should be reassessed. They assert that the most commonly planted weeping willows are actually various hybrids of *Salix babylonica* (which is probably the most beautiful willow but is hardy only in the lower half of the United States), *Salix alba* (most of them open and loose in habit, with some varieties showing red twig color when young and others yellowish most of their lives), and *Salix fragilis.* "There may, indeed, be some weeping willows in our arboreta and nurseries that are superior to most of the others," the scientists conclude. "If so, we should be propagating them, naming, and using them. If nothing else, we should know what to expect when we purchase and plant a tree of a particular cultivar."

🍃 But a weeping willow by any other varietal name is just as beautiful. Sitting underneath such a tree and surveying the passing show, one has the comforting sensation of being screened and sheltered by a curtain of pencil-thin twigs, as soft and as supple as a jumping rope, reaching a length of ten feet, and often trailing on the ground. Covered with smooth, slender leaves as long as seven inches and less than an inch across, the twigs are seldom still. They quiver and flutter in the lightest breeze, and a bunch of them will swing in unison and rise high up in the air if the wind is strong.

🍃 The usually upright trunk is unfortunately prone to cracking, and the branches, as thick as a human arm and thrusting out in every direction, are brittle. A mature seventy-foot specimen often looks like a fibrous ruin. But the twigs that cascade from the top and sides of the gray trunk and gray branches always seem to be plentiful, even when the trunk is more of a stump than what horticulturists call a central leader. Depending on the variety, the twigs have smooth bark that comes in colors ranging from a golden haze to streaks of vivid red and even purplish red, from bright lime green to misty grayish silver.

🍃 All willows, including the dwarf and nonpendulous types, require a lot of water, and for centuries Dutch farmers have planted them on banks of moist soil, often in areas wrested from the sea, to anchor the soil. From a practical as well as esthetic point of view, willows are ideal next to a creek or a pond and will do well in a damp, low spot few other plants can endure. During winter, a gaunt gray weeping willow is a Wordsworthian image as it stands, festooned with twigs in the colors of an apricot, leaning over a blue-gray frozen pond and with the moon hanging in between its decaying branches.

🍃 Besides weeping willows, nurseries and catalogs offer fine varieties of weeping birches, crab apples, lindens, and ornamental cherries. A rare pendulous tree that dominates an area in England's famous Sissinghurst Castle garden is the Silver Frost Weeping Pear. It is spectacular with its abundant foliage of drooping silvery-gray leaves that look like those of a weeping willow but with a profusion of white flowers that resemble those of the finest ornamental pear tree.

⬥ After a survey of trees in terms of shape, one may go back to basics and ask: Might there be a need—and room—for a tree as imposing, if not monumental, as a horse chestnut, with a broad, highly arched crown and with an eventual height of up to a hundred feet and a trunk that may one day measure fifty to sixty inches across?

⬥ For some aficionados, the principal attraction of the horse chestnut tree lies in its sturdy yet subtle panicles of candle-shaped blossoms, in pure white or in bright red, as tall as twelve inches, which appear in great numbers in May and June, or July, and sometimes even later. For others, the horse chestnut is a venerable shade tree, a tree lover's tree: gnarled and knobby, with a thick, coarse bark and branches as randomly sequenced as a family argument. The leaf, which children like to collect, can grow as large as a shovel and is divided into at least five lobes which suggest the fingers of a human hand.

⬥ There are now smaller, cultivated varieties of the traditional horse chestnut, which came originally from the hillsides of the Balkans, and its American cousin, the buckeye. The Bottlebrush Buckeye is a mound-shaped tree, which is often classified as a shrub because its height is between eight and ten feet. What makes this variety of horse chestnut remarkable is its width: as much as fifteen feet. Covered with white flowers in July, this rarely seen but much praised plant can take a partly shaded location, and it is an excellent choice for tough, problematic situations such as a slope.

⬥ The Ruby Horse Chestnut is a hybrid that seldom grows beyond a height of fifty feet and has bright red flowers that set off its dark green foliage.

⬥ Regardless of the size and the variety, the horse chestnut is an exceptionally handsome, stately tree, dense with foliage and not choosy about soil, as long as the drainage is good and the location is reasonably sunny. Its prickly husk contains a fruit that looks like the chestnut we eat roasted in the fall and winter. Unfortunately, the horse chestnut is poisonous to human beings. However, there are now sterile varieties of the traditional basic horse chestnut tree, such as the Double Flowering Horse Chestnut that produces fully double flowers without following them up with nuts.

❧ Landscape architects call the one tree or shrub that dominates your space a specimen plant. It may serve as the centerpiece when set in the lawn or in a flower bed or by a body of water, and it should be given pride of place. Whether redesigning what was someone else's garden or starting from an empty lot that the builder hurriedly covered with strips of sod, it makes good sense to begin by finding such a tree first. At least once in a lifetime, one should enjoy the satisfaction of choosing one's own tree.

5
A Gathering of Flowering Trees

A flowering tree combines the best of both worlds: a stately tree that provides more and more shade—and privacy—as the years pass, as well as the kind of beauty and abundance of blooms that perennial flowers offer.

❧ Nevertheless, when choosing a tree for planting in the home garden, only a small percentage of people focus on the advantages of flowering trees. This is particularly true in the fall, which is the ideal season to plant trees and shrubs. Perhaps the problem is that most flowering trees show their stuff in the spring and the summer, and by the time fall arrives, the immediate inspiration that comes from seeing them in their finest moments is no longer there.

❧ One prominent exception is the crape myrtle, which is perhaps the most popular flowering tree of late summer, with a display that can extend to early fall. Its large, showy panicles—in shades of pink and red, as well as lavender—weigh down the slender branches. The blooms resemble lilacs—and "summer lilac" is another name for crape myrtle.

❧ Technically, the crape myrtle is classified as a shrub because its natural form has a tangle of trunks rather than a single trunk, which defines a tree. However, the crape myrtle is often pruned to develop a single trunk and can be easily trained to adopt such a formal tree form.

ॐ Far less frequently planted is the witch hazel, which is not only believed to have magical properties—its twigs are traditionally used in water divining—but has a most unusual blooming schedule. While the native Virginian witch hazel is the last tree or shrub to bloom in the fall, the Chinese version flowers during winter, often on Christmas Day, and the blooms are golden yellow, brilliant on bare branches. Moreover, the hybrid called Arnold's Promise offers its scented, ribbonlike, deep yellow flowers in February, producing the first bloom of the year.

ॐ The witch hazel is a good choice for a smaller garden and for informal arrangements. Another advantage is its resistance to pollution and other urban stresses.

ॐ Another early-flowering is the serviceberry, also known as shadblow and shadbush because it comes into bloom at the time of the running of the shad in the northeastern United States. The tree is slender and airy, with white and delicate flowers. The serviceberry has also been described as otherworldly—partly because it is mist-like, and partly because in colonial days its blooming coincided with the early spring funeral services held for those who had died during the winter when the ground was thought to be too frozen to dig a grave.

ॐ In the American South particularly, the most popular flowering tree is the evergreen, native magnolia. Its white or creamy blooms are nothing short of voluptuous, and its petals look as if they were made of the lightest silk. But appearances are deceptive. The magnolia is a tough tree that can withstand pollution and neglect, insects and fungi. Its weak point is its eagerness to bud and bloom after the first few balmy days of early spring—and the result is often a withering of the blooms following a return of icy weather.

ॐ One flowering tree that was much in favor around the turn of the century and deserves a comeback is the horse chestnut, and its American cousin, the buckeye, which is still well liked in the Midwest. The upright spikes, called candles by their aficionados, are ethereal, and there are hundreds of them on a mature tree, emerging out of dense foliage. A fairly recent variety praised by botanists is the hybrid Briotii, which offers crimson blooms. The European varieties, which can reach a height above a hundred feet, have white or creamy blooms, while those of the much shorter buckeyes are pink and fragrant.

&. The golden-rain tree is a spectacular plant, grown in some of the great gardens of the world. The golden-yellow flowers come out in late June and dazzle until mid- or even late July. Yet another advantage of this tree, which reaches a height of forty-five feet, is that it will grow well in almost any type of soil.

&. Flowering fruit trees have fascinated the Chinese and the Japanese ever since the beginning of their civilizations. An uncountable number of centuries ago, the Chinese chose as their botanical emblem the apricot blossom, which is sometimes called the plum blossom even though it is an apricot, according to Edwin T. Morris's seminal (Charles Scribner's Sons, 1983) book, *The Gardens of China*. Their decision was based on the fact that apricot blossoms are not only the first ones to appear in the spring, thus breaking winter's spell, but also on the observation that their petals are enduring: They defy the chilly winds of early spring and do not wither before they fall.

&. But the true essence of beauty is in its fleeting nature, the Japanese disciples of Chinese esthetes have come to believe. The precedent the Japanese went back to took place some fifteen hundred years ago, when the Emperor Richiu found "the perfect pleasure" in a moment when petals from an overhanging cherry tree fluttered into his wine cup while he was being rowed around a lake on a boat.

&. The variety Japan sent to the American capital earlier this century as a thoughtful gift is the Yoshino Cherry (*Prunus yedoensis*). Its light pink blossoms are single and fragrant, and they fade to white. The petals are supernally delicate, yet some of them have been known to survive the surprises of a Washington spring for as long as a week.

❧ The tree is upright, with a fine horizontal spread, and the foliage turns an attractive yellow in the fall. It can reach the height of fifty feet.

❧ The Yoshino cherry has two important characteristics: It likes acid soil and it accepts a semi-sunny location. And all cherry trees, ornamental or fruit-bearing, have the advantage of accepting pruning, even heavy pruning, which is best done while they are dormant in winter. Even an old cherry tree with several rotting branches may be rejuvenated by cutting it back severely.

❧ Closely related to the Yoshino is Akebono, which has pink flowers that can withstand far more cold and wind than the Yoshino, and the Weeping Yoshino Cherry, often called Shidare Yoshino. Another close relative is Ivensii, with fragrant white flowers in such quantities that they render the pendulous branches nearly invisible.

❧ Americans unconcerned with Japanese tradition usually opt for robust flowering cherries only distantly related to the fey Yoshino. Two of the most popular among them are the spectacular double-flowering varieties of *Prunus serrulata*, either sold as Kwanzan or, sometimes, as Sekiyama, which is a strong, lasting pink, and Shirofugen (or Shiro-fugan), which offers the unusual show of pink buds which open to white and then fade back to pink. Both flower later than the Yoshino, even later than plum trees, and thus are unlikely to be nipped by frost. Kwanzan has deep dark green foliage which in the fall turns a unique shade of bronze-orange which frequently becomes orange-red. Shirofugen is one of the fastest growing cherry trees.

❧ For a small garden, there is Mount Fuji (also known as Shirotae) which grows only fifteen feet high but can spread horizontally twenty feet across. The buds are pink and open white, and the blossoms are semi-double or double, fragrant and larger than those of other varieties.

🍂 For gardeners who like deep pink, as opposed to light pink, a good choice is the variety sold as Sargent Cherry. The blossoms are single but come in clusters, and the leaves turn to a beautiful bronze-red in the fall. Yet another advantage is a bark with a tint that is between cinnamon and chestnut. An upright shade tree, Sargent Cherry can grow to a height of fifty feet, with a width that is almost equal. However, this variety also has a slender columnar form which is unfortunately seldom available commercially.

🍂 Like other ornamental fruit trees, flowering cherry trees produce fruits, which are mostly pits covered with a bitter tasting skin. But birds of all types like them. The idea of selecting and hybridizing fruit trees for the beauty and abundance of their blossoms rather than the tastiness of their fruits is believed to be either Chinese or Japanese in origin, and in both civilizations, history records that emperors and imperial administrators either rewarded or plundered the choice trees of their subjects.

🍂 Once you have planted a flowering tree, there is a new way to measure time: things come to be remembered as having happened either before or after the tree bloomed, and a certain year comes to be known as the one in which the blooms were more than usually numerous or beautiful. Some gardeners go as far as planting several flowering trees and then set their social calendar so their friends may also admire those grand blooms that have the sky as their backdrop. Emperor Richiu's pursuit of the perfect moment endures.

6
The Color Yellow

On the Washington, D.C., street where I lived for nineteen years, there is one spreading maple two stories high that prompts passersby to stop and motorists to slow down every October, after its masses of leaves turn an amazing yellow overnight, a color that stays unchanged until the leaves wither and drop a few weeks later. The tint is more vivid than the amber of wheat stalks after harvest, but not quite as brilliant as the sunflower's yellow, which hovers on the verge of orange.

❧ Throughout spring and summer, gardeners have a lingering suspicion that yellow foliage is a sign of a plant's poor health. The term "sickly yellow" is used much too often to describe a shrub or a tree that does not display the kind of rich, dark green that proves the abundant presence of chlorophyll, the complex, indispensable chemical that with the assistance of sunshine converts carbon dioxide and water into carbohydrates, the daily food of plants. However, chlorophyll is also present in plants that normally have yellow foliage during spring and summer, and a splash of yellow can provide a pleasant contrast to the ubiquitous mass of green.

❧ Healthy, respectable yellow-leafed varieties of plants—often easy to tell by their botanical names, which feature the Latin word for golden, *aureum* or *aurea*—exist in surprisingly large numbers. Their list includes such favorites as cypress, arborvitae, mock orange, ligustrum, barberry, and marjoram. An elderberry called Aurea has leaves with a loud shade of yellow that is not far from chromium. The berries are black and the contrast between the two colors is attractive. Another elderberry, *Plumosa aurea*, has yellow leaves that turn yellow-green by the end of the summer, and its berries are scarlet. A form of honey locust aptly named Sunburst is a quick-growing, handsome tree with golden-yellow leaves which turn greenish yellow by late summer. A graceful, airy Japanese maple called Aureum, famous for its horizontal layers of branches that suggest steps, starts out in the spring with greenish yellow leaves that become a sunny, medium yellow by midsummer.

🍂 Nevertheless, yellow foliage is undoubtedly the most dramatic after it turns from ordinary green in the fall. Among trees showing lovely yellows in the fall, maples—with a spectrum ranging from orange-red through carmine to reddish purples—are the star performers. Japanese maples, particularly Okushimo which grows about six feet tall, offer brilliant, almost sulfur yellow.

🍂 Except for Bonfire, all sugar maples turn yellow, and one of the best among them is Goldspire—narrow, conical in shape—which is transformed from leathery dark green to a lustrous rich yellow. The even more slender sugar maple called Monumentale has mellow orange-yellow foliage.

🍂 In the top three on any list of trees with great fall color is the maple Red Sunset. Its soft orange-red comes out early and is a guaranteed show-stopper, appearing some three weeks before October Glory, which is another maple appreciated for its color: a triumphant, nearly uniform crimson. While many red maples do not develop strong fall colors unless planted in good soil and on favorable sites with plenty of sun—and they also tend to drop their leaves fairly early—Red Sunset and October Glory are not so finicky, and October Glory is a champion in managing to keep its leaves for a long time, often until the end of November.

❧ In two years out of three, sugar maples—also known as rock maples and hard maples—offer stunning combinations of yellows, oranges, and reds. But the colors and their degree of brilliance vary significantly from one year to the next, with their beauty depending on high contrasts between night and day temperatures as well as on sufficient moisture. The cultivar Bonfire, which was selected for its fast growth, also happens to have a more reliably dazzling color display—its hue is carmine.

❧ There are several mountain-ash varieties that offer golden-yellow foliage as well as clusters of berries of the same color. The variety called Aurea or Yellow White Beam is considered one of the best, with leaves and berries staying on until late fall.

❧ For a steady, clear yellow, a popular choice is the thornless honey locust, and Shademaster is one of the best varieties. While tolerant of drought and producing dappled shade acceptable to lawn grasses, most locusts lose their leaves early.

❧ The tulip tree—a giant reaching 150 feet and bearing green-and-yellow tuliplike flowers in early to late spring—also delivers a fine yellow that in some years deepens into a fabulous gold. Robust, with branches spreading far horizontally, the tulip tree is for a large, spacious yard.

❧ Another spectacular producer of fall yellow is the gingko. Also known as the maidenhair tree and considered one of the world's oldest trees, it has a sturdy, pillarlike trunk and requires virtually no pruning. It is a good tree for city gardens and streets because its columnar shape, much like the Lombardy poplar's, fits into narrow, small spaces. The variety known as Princeton Sentry resembles the Lombardy poplar most, but it does not have the Lombardy poplar's habit of sprouting gangs of suckers and fracturing in a storm. There is also a fine pendulous gingko that is rarely seen, but no gingko is a true shade tree; all of its varieties are too emphatically vertical. It is at its most effective when two rows of them are lined up as an allée along a long driveway.

🍂 Gingkos resist pollution and insects, and qualify as an ideal urban tree. The female of the species produces pecks of fruit that people in the Far East consider a delicacy, but most others are repelled by the penetrating smell, which can easily be mistaken for the smell of chicken manure. Male gingkos do not bear fruit, and that is the tree that nurseries sell. Because of its dense, fibrous roots, gingko is one of the least problematic trees to transplant.

🍂 The lower part of the gingko's trunk is usually bare, but the upper part is draped in dense layers of fan-shaped leaves with curved edges, the size of a silver dollar, that turn from a medium green to a clear golden yellow after the first night that slips under fifty degrees Fahrenheit. The leaves are unusually numerous, and after they fall off, the ground gleams and glistens as if covered with gold coins.

🍂 Most gingko varieties are slow growers in the first few years. They are tall and slender for a decade or so, then they broaden and acquire a pyramid shape.

🍂 The native American dogwood, *Cornus florida,* must be mentioned in any discussion of fall color. In fact, the parade of turning leaves traditionally begins with the dogwood's splashes of deep, rich crimson over a lively green background. However, the sad news is that a fungus called *Discula anthracnose* is killing the native American dogwood not only from the north to the south but from east to west as well, with no antidote in sight. Dogwoods attacked by the fungus have a nearly one hundred percent fatality rate, and victims have been found not only in the great contiguous woods from Maine to Florida, where the fungus was first spotted, but within city limits as well. "The march of that fungus is inexorable," says Frank Santamour, the National Arboretum's tree specialist. Others point to a few isolated specimens that have survived and hope that by studying them, we may find some resistant strains.

🍂 The good news is that the Oriental variety, *Cornus kousa,* is resistant—though not immune—to the fungus, as are some of the other dogwood varieties. Efforts are under way in various laboratories to produce hybrids that will keep the advantages of *Cornus florida* and resist the fungus.

&. Nearly every year, the sassafras, a native American tree, offers a brilliant, long-lasting royal scarlet, with orange as its undertone. But like another great fall red, the American sweet gum, the sassafras is difficult to transplant. The long taproot seems to be the reason for that problem, and it is best not to transplant these two trees if they exceed two feet in height.

&. The achievement of noteworthy fall color is not a characteristic precisely encoded in the gene of each species. Both the coloring and the leaves' staying power are significantly affected by annual fluctuations in temperature and moisture levels, as well as by variations in site and soil. What seems to matter most is not the species but the individual tree, and some can be relied upon to offer vivid hues year after year, regardless of changing circumstances. However, unfortunately to those who would like to pick a tree with one particular tint, we usually find about the leaves true fall color only after planting the sapling.

&. The turning of leaves is as admirable a spectacle as the clusters of pretty petals unfolding during spring and summer. Yet oddly enough, few people choose their trees on the basis of fall display; nor do hybridizers cross trees in order to get the finest leaf colors for autumn. In the botanical marketplace, where improvement on the natural is the chief guiding principle, hybridizers usually work toward objectives such as a smaller or larger size, a broader or narrower shape, tolerance of drought or pollution, a particular bloom color or petal structure or a denser foliage.

&. If red is the dominant tint of flame, suggesting surging, irrepressible passion, then yellow is the color of embers burning slowly. Yellow is the color that bespeaks such sentiments as deep respect and quiet resignation, affectionate remembrance and unrequited love. Fading well, yellow is a color of Proustian grace. It is the color for romantics.

7
Tall, Straight, and Narrow

Y ou have an asphalt driveway or a flagstone-paved path leading to the house. You have seen other people accent such passages by planting on both sides trees with a nice horizontal spread, such as cherries upright or weeping, or crab apples or maples of various types.

🍂 But no, your mind is set on slender, classical columns—the slimmer the better. You are drawn to the clear, uncluttered lines of trees tapering to a narrow point, with erect and parallel branches. Or you are simply being practical: you don't want trees to take up too much space on a small city lot. You do want trees, oh yes, but they should be shaped like exclamation points and form a neat row.

🍂 A tree that fills such a bill is described as *fastigiate,* an elegant mouthful of a Latinate term, a dictionary neighbor to such words as "fascicle" (bundle) and "fast" (in the sense of firm and steadfast). In short, a fastigiate tree is tall, straight, and narrow. And my unscientific survey suggests that such a tree is for the chosen fastidious few rather than for what Marxists call the broad masses.

🍂 The best-known tree that sums up that definition is the Lombardy poplar, one of the great, memorable trees of the European landscape, which stands guard to the approaches to grand estates and lines countless country roads. Lombardy poplars shoot up to a height of ninety feet, and when planted next to a ditch that channels overflow rainwater, they may grow as fast as four feet a year, which qualifies them as one of the world's fastest growing trees.

🍂 Around the turn of the century, Lombardy poplars were planted in large numbers in the United States. They did not fare well in our climate, which is wetter and more violent than Europe's. However, to this day, some nurseries keep selling them as "a choice tree" that "grows incredibly fast in any soil."

🍂 The unpleasant truth is that the Lombardy poplar frequently acquires a canker as it matures, and the canker, which is untreatable, kills the top. Though lower parts of the tree stay alive, such a tree is unsightly. But even if the tree somehow escapes the ravages of the canker, it grows too fast for its cells to develop a dense structure leading to a sturdy frame. If you plant the trees in a row, a storm will soon snap one trunk in two, and the next storm may break another. The symmetry is broken, and there is no way to repair it. Removing a damaged Lombardy poplar creates yet another problem: the roots are extra vigorous and they keep sending up shoots, undiscouraged by attempts to cut them off as soon as they emerge.

🍂 Lombardy poplar roots search for moisture, which they need more than most other trees, and often the only place where they can find it is in waterpipes and sewers, which they encircle with their roots and then crack and shatter.

🍂 For all these reasons it is best to say no to the Lombardy poplar. Horticulturists recommend Lombardy poplars to commercial developers and builders of industrial sites only as an emergency measure—to provide a temporary screen in a hurry.

🍂 In structure and size, a variety of gingko called Sentry comes closest to the Lombardy poplar. Like other gingkos, Sentry is long-lived and immune to pests and diseases. Its straight, sturdy trunk resists high winds and needs no corrective staking.

🍂 Among maples, the narrowest are Temple Upright, Newton Sentry, and Erectum. Yet another recommended variety is the Sentry sugar maple.

🍂 The usually broad, much-beloved English oak, *Quercus robur,* has a recommended variety called Fastigiata, as does the European beech. Though dogwoods have a strong horizontal spreading habit, there is one dogwood that is reliably slender, a variety called Fastigiata.

🍂 Some trees are narrow and columnlike only when they are young. As the years pass and their lateral branches grow stronger and longer, they acquire a middle-age spread. They may also bend under the burden of their fruits or as a result of a storm, and they need help—staking—to spring back to their original upright positions. One tree that needs such help is a fine birch called Fastigiata.

🍂 If the objective is to have an allée or a windbreak of a certain height, homeowners and park-keepers often cut off the tops at a certain level. In other circumstances, such "topping off" would be a mistake, even a mortal sin against the tree. But in case of fastigiate trees that need to be controlled, horticulturists regard the action as permissible.

🍂 A graceful columnar tree that fills out a little in about ten years or so is a European or littleleaf linden called Greenspire. It is a lovely tree with an emphatically upright, pyramidal growth and a straight trunk that does not need to be staked. Eventually, the tight columnar form becomes slightly oval. (Linden flowers have a spicy fragrance that is beloved by honeybees.)

🍂 Among evergreens, the most spectacular fastigiate tree, highly prized in formal Mediterranean gardens, is a variety of Italian cypress called Stricta. Unfortunately, Stricta is not reliably hardy in the upper two-thirds of the United States.

🍂 Another variety called Stricta is an Irish yew, which can reach a height of thirty feet, but will fill out in the middle eventually.

🍃 A hardier tree that looks much like Stricta is the California incense-cedar, which grows up to a height of thirty feet yet keeps its girth to two to four feet.

🍃 Junipers and arborvitaes, columnlike in most cases, have several admirable varieties with a tight, narrowly columnar shape bred into them. White pine too has a variety called Fastigiata. But white pine's proclivity for a horizontal spread does eventually overtake every mature Fastigiata. The lacy, elegant Lawson False Cypress, increasingly popular among gardeners nationwide, has a number of excellent fastigiate varieties such as Allumii, Erecta, and Fletcheri. They all do well and do not fill out after their youth is gone. But they do not grow beyond twenty feet. The shortest, Allumii, stops around six feet.

🍃 If windstorms and snowstorms are frequent in your area, it might be wiser to choose a fastigiate variety that does not grow too tall and does not present a target for high winds.

🍃 Shopping around for fastigiate trees does usually take extra time. Not all nurseries and mail order houses carry them. But even if they are in stock, a large order from a city or a park often depletes local resources. It is best to start inquiries and to file orders early, many weeks before the fall or spring planting season begins.

A Gallery of Trees

8
The Wisdom of Birches

Birches swaying in the wind demonstrate the grace and the power of a bending stalk. They beckon to us—our eyes follow their motion as they make their compromises with the fiercest winds. Birches bend rather than break, even if that means nearly prostrating themselves on the ground.

❧ The time we can best witness the wisdom of birches is in a storm, as we watch how a dignified, robust, straight-trunked oak or an energetically multibranched maple is straining to stay erect. These trees defy the wind while creaking and groaning, occasionally dropping a branch or a twig that died or was damaged some time ago, or suddenly snapping in two with a loud report, which can be as frightening as watching a person being hit by a bullet.

❧ While oaks and maples are among the first casualties of hurricanes, birches usually survive intact.

❧ The birch, *beth* in ancient Celtic, is the first in the druidic alphabet of trees and one of the first forest trees in the Old World to leaf out in the spring. Herbal lore speaks of extracts from birch bark as a salve for chafed skin and aching joints. Throughout pagan Europe, birch rods were used in ceremonies to drive out the spirit of the old year, as the birch stands for the

Birch

first month of the lunar year that begins after the winter solstice. It is the tree of inception, regarded as a sign of encouragement for lovers.

🍂 A single birch, even if multitrunked, looks lost and forlorn; a clump of closely planted trees, however, lends an air of distinction to a small townhouse courtyard without overwhelming it. A stand of birches along the driveway or by the footpath leading to the house admirably breaks up the solid green expanse of a suburban lawn without disturbing lawn grasses the least bit.

🍂 To grow birches in clumps, plant two, three, or even four saplings ten to fifteen inches apart in the same large hole and tilt each trunk slightly outward. Some gardeners use stakes and wires to make sure that the young and pliable—in fact, too pliable—birch trunks grow in the desired directions. But the stakes must be removed eventually because their straightness interferes with the harmony of the gently bending birch trunks.

🍂 To train birches to develop a multitrunk structure, cut a young tree to the ground and select the most vigorous fresh shoots to become the new trunks. One may engage in such radical pruning at any time of the year. But it is wise to refrain from any pruning—except to remove broken or diseased branches—from midspring to late summer, when growth is the strongest and any cuts made are likely to bleed profusely.

🍂 The best time to plant birches is in early spring, when the soil begins to feel soft again. Since it is a tree that is not easy to transplant, insist on its being properly balled-and-burlapped. Birches of all varieties grow best in loam, but they will accept clayey soil, particularly if it is loosened up with plenty of sand, peat moss, leaf mold, compost, or fine topsoil. Their only stringent requirement is one inch of water a week if there is no rain.

🍂 Even for those who have precise ideas—or insistent memories—of the birches they want to plant, it is a good idea to survey the broad range of varieties available nowadays through nurseries and mail order catalogs. There are fine native

North American birches, as well as others that originated in the northern regions of Asia and Europe. There are also plenty of new and improved varieties.

❦ The most popular native birch, widespread in the open woods and riverbanks of northeastern North America, is the canoe birch or paper birch, classified botanically as *Betula papyrifera.* Also known as white birch—a term sometimes applied generically to all white-barked birches—the canoe birch has been used by the Indians for their birchbark canoes as well as their baskets and trays. The trunk is silky smooth and chalky white, and its bark, striped dark gray or black, peels off in large sheets. Given a favorable environment, it can grow up to one hundred feet. The horizontal branches are long and numerous, the twigs thin and droopy.

❦ No more than sixty feet in height is the European birch most popular on this continent, *Betula pendula,* also known as *Betula alba* or *Betula verrucosa.* With chalky white trunk and branches, this European import has a pyramidal structure and slightly pendulous lateral branches.

❦ Unfortunately, birches have a deadly enemy, the bronze birch borer. It is more likely to attack—and sometimes kill—the European birch than the native species. DDT was once widely used to control the borer, a flat-headed grub between half an inch and one inch in length, which devours the tree just under the bark. Dieldrin is the spray used nowadays, and it has to be applied at least three times each May and June.

❦ Regardless of the borers, the improved varieties developed out of the European birch are most tempting: Fastigiata, which is slender and columnar in shape; Cutleaf European Birch, which has a graceful, pendulous habit; Purple Splendor, which has spectacular purple foliage; and Scarlet Glory, which has leaves red in the spring and in the fall, and reddish green during the summer.

❦ Young's Weeping Birch is an outstanding variety in the weeping mode. Its lower branches touch the ground, and the leaves, unusually plentiful for a birch, turn an intriguing shade of greenish gold before they fall. Thus it is only during winter that one notices the dramatic silvery white of the bark.

❧ Among birches of Asian origin, the Chinese Paper Birch has a bark that keeps shredding and shedding—an activity botanists call exfoliating; the bark colors range from bright orange to orange-red. According to the authoritative *Wyman's Gardening Encyclopedia,* no other tree has such bark.

❧ Somewhat similar in its colors and in its exfoliating habit is a recently developed cultivar of the river birch called Heritage, which is said to be highly resistant to the bronze birch borer. In 1990, Heritage headed the list of the Styer Award of Garden Merit, an annual selection of outstanding plants for the mid-Atlantic region, as judged by leading horticulturists and nursery owners. Heritage's bark, which keeps peeling off, ranges in color from salmon pink to grayish, including a tint of cinnamon. The foliage is glossy green which turns a pleasant shade of yellow in the fall, which is what the majority of birches do.

❧ The bark of birches pales with age, and the mysterious markings on the bark that resemble runic writing become more pronounced.

❧ When choosing a birch, pay particular attention to the parts of the country where it is recommended. The European white birch is for areas where the temperature dips at least -20° Fahrenheit; south of this area, sooner or later it is likely to be attacked by the bronze birch borer, which starts at the top of the tree so that its penetration is hard to notice. Once inside the bark, the borer will tunnel through the tree's vital structures and thrive on its sap, which is a sweetish liquid that humans ferment and make into birch beer. The tree that bends so artfully and wisely with the wind cannot stand up to the borer consuming it from the inside.

❧ The native American river birch is more likely to survive borers than other birches. Location matters too. Open, colder, windswept areas are less likely to be invaded by the borer than cozy, warmer, built-up urban and suburban settings.

❧ There are two more reasons to be hopeful. The first is that in neighborhoods without birches it may take several years before borers make their appearance. Second, robust birches that are watered every week and are growing in enriched soil with improved drainage, are less likely to succumb to the borers than puny saplings plunked down in a thin layer of improved soil.

❧ Most people plant birches because of their fond memories of birch forests. For Robert Frost, bent birch trunks suggested a lonely child who had been swinging on them, taking the stiffness out until "not one but hung limp, not one was left/For him to conquer." For Poles and Russians, birches are a beloved constant of their landscapes, and they think of the tree as graceful and feminine—and as melancholy as life itself in that part of the world.

9
The Grandeur of Oak

Of all the trees on earth, the oak is one that can make the human heart quiver.

• There are other magnificent trees: the redwoods and sequoias of the American West, the banyans of India, the baobabs of Africa. But the oak has been the glory tree of the Old World. Abraham played host to angels under a tree thought to be an oak, and King Arthur's round table of fellowship was made of that most royal of woods. And when in the end a lovely maiden cast a spell on the magician Merlin, she imprisoned him in a hollow oak.

• An oak trunk is straight and massive, bringing to the mind a column in a colonnade, the mast of a ship, an axis, a fulcrum. Equally impressive is the spread and the spacing of an oak's lateral branches, which suggest the harmonious proportions of a Greek temple of antiquity. Even the oak's Latin name, *quercus,* sounds patrician.

• Size too contributes to an image of grandeur. Few species of oak will stay under the height of fifty feet, and some, like the shumard oak and the black oak, will not stop growing at the height of one hundred feet, and the horizontal spread can be even greater. According to Virgil, the great poet of Roman antiquity, the oak's roots burrow as deep into the earth as its

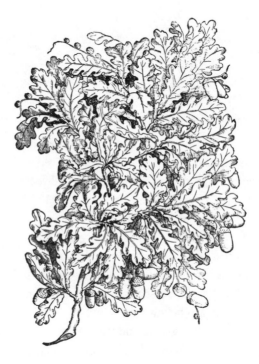

Common Oak

branches soar into the sky. According to Robert Graves, that span "makes it emblematic of a god whose law runs both in Heaven and in the Underworld." It was said in the ancient Mediterranean world that the oak's trunk "courts the lightning flash," and the oak was sacred to Zeus and Jupiter, and to the chief gods of the Germanic and Celtic pantheons.

❧ In our day, garden design is in the throes of a romantic revival, and the oak is a tree that fits into that mood. But it is a good idea to look around for the most suitable varieties. An oak is for a large yard, and we must be careful in plotting out how far its crown will eventually extend.

❧ One person may be awed by the pyramid-shaped pin oak, with branches growing so low that they touch the ground. This is the tall, slender tree that graces the grounds of the White House and the U.S. Capitol. But another person may be inspired by the reach of the horizontal limbs of a live oak, which start near the base of a broad trunk. Beloved in the South where it does not drop its leaves in the winter—hence its popular description as "live"—this is one oak with a spread that can be twice its height, which is about sixty feet.

❧ A slow grower, the white oak is a native American, a mainstay of the forests of the eastern United States and the source of timber for flooring, furniture, and ships. White oaks have a broad, round crown and an open structure that enables electrical wires to pass freely in between their branches.

❧ Oak leaves are roughly symmetrical, but the lobe arrangements of various species look as if they had been designed by artists as different as the classical master of detail Albrecht Dürer (scarlet oak) and the playful twentieth-century painter Georges Braque (English oak). The southern red oak has a narrow, irregular leaf that looks like a child's attempt to draw a lance; the white oak's leaf is the closest to the idealized oak leaf that many armies have chosen for their medals to symbolize bravery under fire.

❧ The oak leaf's most characteristic feature is an indentation that differs from species to species. One exception is the leaf of the willow oak, which is long and slender, much like a willow leaf and without any indentation.

❧ Most oak species will turn red in the fall—some blood red, others close to purple. Named after its brilliant foliage is the scarlet oak, which is the official tree of the District of Columbia and is planted throughout the nation's capital. On the other hand, the shingle oak has fall foliage that offers a hue of yellow-bronze.

❧ The oak's fruit is the acorn, an intriguing design for a seed, which also shows an amazing variation in shape and size. Children like to collect them, hogs devour them, and American Indians have dried them and made a flour that was baked into a kind of bread.

❧ Perhaps the principal reason for the appeal of the oak is its solid dignity. While the oak is as much the king of the forest flora as the lion is the king of the fauna, the oak also prompts us to pay it homage when we encounter it on city streets and parks, in country lanes and on estates. In the Old World as well as the New, the oak has been perceived as a botanical icon for the values of longevity, tradition, and majesty. Its Celtic name, *duir,* is cognate with "door" in many Indo-European languages, which may be related to the Hebrew letter *daleth,* which is the same word for door, and having some connection with the fact that the stoutest doors of antiquity were made of oak. Robert Graves calls the oak "a tree of endurance and triumph." It is a tree that one looks up to in every sense of the word.

10
The Workaday Maple

Whether for a minuscule townhouse front yard, a spacious suburban estate, or a treebox of a city street, the maple tree is a wise choice. Its many varieties fit different environments and purposes, with its shapes including the round and the wide-spreading, the low-mounded, and the tall and columnar. Its leaves may be simply lobed or ornately compounded, but their common denominator is a robust, leafy presence. The genus *Acer* is remarkably tolerant of fumes from the internal combustion engine and resistant to most insects and fungi.

❧ Some maples such as the Norway maple and the red maple offer a dense canopy and full shade, and most maples have fine and often spectacular fall colors. The sap of the sugar maple—as well as the sap of some other maples—provides a syrup with a great flavor as distinctive as chocolate's and coffee's, though not as popular.

❧ There are about 200 maple species. China leads with fifty-nine, North America follows with twenty-five, then comes Japan, with sixteen. Europe trails behind with only thirteen species it can call its own. While maples can be found thriving as far north as Alaska and Siberia, a few species have also been spotted in the tropics.

Norway Maple

❧ Most maples native to North America and Europe grow fast in their first few years, as much as three feet a year. But after they reach the height of fifteen feet, they slow down and increase only about one foot a year.

❧ On the other hand, Japanese maples form a category of their own, seldom growing above the height of twenty feet. Their growth is usually exceedingly slow. Perhaps their genetic makeup is determined by their inability to grow taller on the archipelago's rocky soil, thus they developed into a compact species, but the experts are uncertain if that is indeed the case. Nor is there an explanation for the appearance in Japan of maples with leaves with as many as eleven lobes, some of them most intricately divided and lacelike, as if designed by a master painter of Japan, and with colors ranging from the usual shades of green all the way to yellows, pinks, and reds, and including combinations of these colors as well.

❧ A European maple that deserves more attention is the hedge maple (*Acer campestre*), which is highly recommended as a low-growing tree, ideal under overhead electric wires, and with a dense, vigorous growth that is easily sheared. While the variety known as Hedge Maple has corklike bark and a dense, most attractive foliage, another *Acer campestre* variety, Compactum, has the added advantage of being more wide than it is tall. Postelense has leaves that are golden yellow when they come out, then turn green. The toughest selection for use as a street tree is Queen Elizabeth. One disadvantage of *Acer campestre* is that its autumn color does not measure up to the standards of the genus.

❧ Little known and therefore seldom planted in the New World is the Paperbark Maple (*Acer griseum*), which is the one maple that may be planted for its splendid bark, which is cinnamon-colored and peels in strips, much like birch. A native of western China, it is beloved by Chinese gardeners of the classical school. Its height seldom goes over twenty-five feet, and its fall leaf color of coral red further strengthens its candidacy as a dramatic specimen tree.

❧ A tree much in favor across North America is the native red maple (*Acer rubrum*). It gets its name from its bright red flowers, which break out in April, before the leaves appear, or perhaps from the bright red of its "fruits"—propeller-like flattened nuts called samaras—which make their appearance in late spring. The red color returns again in the fall, when the foliage turns a brilliant, royal scarlet. Also known as swamp maple, the red maple likes low-lying, wet, even swampy spots. Because its fast growth results in brittle branches, the naturally occurring "wild" variety of red maple easily sprouting from seed is not recommended for the home ground.

❧ Superior hybrids among red maples include October Glory and Red Sunset, both of them admired for their solid, roughly symmetrical upright structure and their amazing fall display of foliage, with hues of scarlet, orange-red and crimson. The variety Columnare is about half as wide as it is tall.

❧ The maple to avoid is the Silver Maple (*Acer saccharinum*) which shoots up as high as 120 feet and is traditionally planted for shade, or simply allowed to sprout from a stray seed. Though a spreading, storybook-type tree with arching and sometimes pendulous branches, Silver Maple grows much too rapidly and will often splinter and break in wind and ice storms. In its place, purchase named maple cultivars, such as Bonfire, Summershade, and Goldspire.

❧ The most common maple in America is the Norway maple, a native of Europe. Round-headed and densely branched, Norway maples first sprout small yellow flowers in the spring, followed by the leaves, which have five lobes and are about six inches across—the pattern usually identified as the maple leaf—and turn yellow in the fall. Nurseries grow many Norway maple varieties: Cleveland is an oval, Crimson Sentry is columnar, Jade Glen is broad. Among the newer varieties, Goldsworth Purple and Fassens Black keep their red foliage color throughout the growing season. Summer Shade was selected for heat resistance and Globosum for its dense branches and globe shape.

&❦ But scientists are not satisfied with the genealogical charts and the nomenclature of this eminently adaptable—perhaps even too adaptable—genus. According to a specialist in maples, Alden Townsend of the National Arboretum, "the breeding and selecting of maples has been neglected" by botanists, despite the fact that maples offer "great hope," particularly for urban plantings. As a pollution-resistant, many-branched tree of beautiful foliage, the maple represents "a virtually untapped genetic resource," Townsend says.

&❦ In his opinion, the many species and the vast number of their regional variations, many of them occurring naturally, need to be carefully studied and identified, and the most promising saplings selected and further hybridized. He and other students of trees see the maple as the basic workhorse tree of the future, in urban as well as rural settings, for the home ground as well as streets and parks.

&❦ The maple is a plain, workaday tree when compared to the majestic oak acclaimed by Druids and Greeks as the first and foremost among trees, or to the lyrical birch, which conveys mystery and melancholy, or to the long-lived, faithful yew, which stands witness in Christian churchyards and cemeteries. Except for the use of its leaf on the Canadian flag, the maple has no great emblematic or mythological significance. Nevertheless, it has spread across the forests of the northern hemisphere, and in North American suburbs, it is probably planted more frequently than any other tree. On the home ground, the maple is number one.

11
Unsung Trees: Paulownia and Catalpa

T he fragrance is what hits you first—usually in May, but earlier if summer arrives ahead of schedule, as it often does—in locations that are as unexpected as an approach to a bridge smothered with asphalt or a vacant city lot buried under broken bricks and upended sofas. Wafting through the open car window is a scent that is musky, sensual, and unmistakably decadent. It first suggests a lilac, but it is without lilac's clarity of freshness and innocence. If you sniff the blossom up close, the fragrance is heavy, even overwhelming: deeply sweet yet with more than just a hint of incipient putrefaction. One connoisseur, who is intrigued, says she is reminded of the oleander, which is supposed to emit vapors that are enticing but also toxic, so much so that Roman legionnaires were once warned not to sleep in oleander groves. Or at least so claims a legend cited by today's Romans.

• The tree is called paulownia or royal paulownia, named after Anna Pavlovna, whose life spanned the eighteenth and nineteenth centuries and who was the daughter of Czar Paul I of Russia, first a friend and then the enemy of Napoleon. She married into the Dutch royal family. The paulownia is also known as the princess tree and the empress tree.

• Its blossom is trumpet-shaped, two to three inches long;

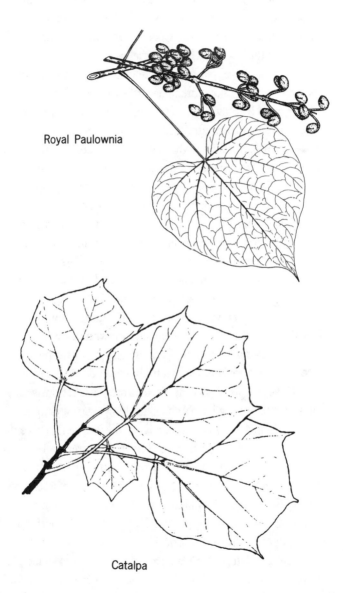

Royal Paulownia

Catalpa

some twenty or even more of them hang downward and make up one soft, airy pyramid as long as fourteen inches. On the outside, the color is a glorious lavender that fades into pale yellow and white inside. The blooms, appearing in clusters, fairly cover the tree, which easily reaches a height of sixty feet, and its asymmetrical tan or gray branches form a broad crown. The flowers are all the more noteworthy because they are accompanied by only a few of the heart-shaped, downy leaves, most of which appear after the flowers are gone.

&. Botanists downgrade the paulownia as "coarse" in branch structure and leaf texture, and one tree specialist dismisses it as "guilty of insufficient delicacy" in general. Gardeners often bracket the paulownia with the catalpa (also called catawba), a tree similar in its quick growth and the readiness of its seedpod to break open, releasing lots of seeds that sprout in unlikely spaces. The two trees have similar branching habits and virtually identical, heart-shaped leaves, which in the catalpa's case can grow as big as a shovel. Like the paulownia, the catalpa is also a showy flowering tree, blooming a few weeks after the paulownia. Catalpa blossoms are white or yellow, and usually marked with specks of yellow, orange, or purple.

&. The catalpa's fame derives from its slender fruit or capsule, as long as twenty inches, that has been variously compared to a string bean or an extra-long cigar. It dangles from the branches by the hundreds and has earned the tree the popular sobriquet "cigar tree" or "Indian cigar tree," a reference to the fact that it is an American native, with a species called Western (and also known as Northern) that only experts can distinguish from the Southern (also known as common) catalpa. One difference is the length of the "cigar"; another is the depth of the furrowed bark. There is also a yellow (sometimes called golden) catalpa, a native of China, which has thinner cigars than those of the American species.

&. The catalpa was discovered by European visitors in the eighteenth century and was exported to the Old World where it was much appreciated for its blooms, which were described as orchidlike, and for its invariably crooked branches that offer a strong visual contrast to the straight, pendulous "cigars" which sway in the wind in appealing unison. Frederick the Great, Voltaire's Prussian patron, planted hundreds of catalpas on his estate in Potsdam toward the middle of the eighteenth century, and many of their descendants are still alive and flourishing.

&. While catalpas thrive for a hundred years and more in the cooler and less humid European climate, they are short-lived in America, where they are good for no more than one human generation, or two at best. Thomas Jefferson is recorded to have been fond of them, and so were many plantation owners in the Deep South as well as some Boston Brahmins.

&. The catalpa's main problem is root rot. More recently, catalpas have been discovered to be allergic to air pollution. But even in Colonial Williamsburg, where the use of automobiles is kept to a minimum, an avenue of catalpas leading to the governor's mansion is part of the reconstructed rather than the genuine past: the trees have been replanted several times since colonial days.

&. The paulownia and the catalpa are sometimes downright condemned as "trash trees," even as weeds, mostly because they grow so fast—as much as twenty feet in the first years of their life, provided they are in the full sun. Their branches sprout out helter-skelter, and they break easily in high winds. Also, they are shallow-rooted, which means that they can be yanked out of the ground in a storm.

&. Few if any nurseries bother to grow paulownias and catalpas. Yet both trees offer advantages to someone who has just bought a house surrounded by grass, but who has no trees and would like some in a hurry. Some gardeners grow them because of their interest in sprouting trees from seeds they personally gathered. Then there are also cases of people falling in love with the paulownia's strange fragrance or with the fairyland sight of the catalpa's cigarlike seedpods dangling from branches.

&. Oddly enough, however, farmers who have tried to grow

paulownia in their fields have not been as successful. There
have been several waves of interest in raising paulownia as a
tree crop, but somehow, paulownias growing in open fields
have not done as well as those in vacant city lots.

&❧ The main source of inspiration has been Japan, where the
paulownia, called *kiri no ki,* is a native and venerated as an
exceptional tree. Young Japanese brides often start out on a
marriage with a trousseau of clogs, boxes, and chests of drawers
made of its wood, which is almost as light as balsa and nearly as
hard as maple. The Japanese appreciate the quality of
paulownia lumber, which will not rot, warp, or split. One
reason for its popularity is that it is said to burn slowly in case
the house catches fire, which until recently was a frequent
disaster in the island nation. When doused with water,
paulownia wood is said to burn even slower.

&❧ Shortly before and during World War II, Americans also
experimented with paulownia in constructing airplanes,
thinking that it might work better than metal. As a veneer,
tissue-thin paulownia has been incorporated in musical
instruments.

&❧ Though fungal infestations cause much damage to the live
wood, properly dried-out and cured catalpa lumber is one of
the best, toughest, and most enduring fence-post materials even
if it is not treated with chemicals. Along with locust, mulberry,
and Osage orange, catalpa is the fencemaker's lumber of choice.

12
Strange Pears

Anyone for a minimum-maintenance, problem-free fruit tree that is also highly ornamental, with masses of cloud-like white blossoms in the spring and the entire foliage turning a brilliant scarlet after the first chilly night of fall? Is anyone interested in planting a fine tree that has proved itself eminently adapted to living in most of the United States?

&❧ A description of such a tree must start with its fruit, ready for eating in the fall. Anne Lazar of Bethesda identified the fruit after the first bite as "that strange pear" of her childhood in France. She remembered that her uncle, a vintner in the Beaujolais region, grew a tree next to the house that he called *poire-coing*—quince pear—to distinguish it from other pears. Ordinary pears had an elegant pear shape and were juicy, soft, and sweet. But the quince pear was formed like an apple and had a tart taste. It was still hard when it was picked, and it softened only after several weeks in storage.

&❧ People who grew up in rural Maryland describe that same pear with a shrug as "just a Maryland pear," and they tend to poor-mouth it for its coarse texture and its mottled beige-brown-gray coloring, which resembles the bark of the sycamore

Pear

tree. Indeed, the Maryland pear does not have the usual fancy variety name, such as Flemish Beauty, Colette, or Red Anjou, and it grows wild in some parts of the state.

&❧ There are several versions of the Maryland pear. One begins to ripen in September, and another in October. Yet another is still hard as a rock in November. Its rough texture eventually softens by the New Year, but only if the pears are picked before the first frost and are then stored in a dry, cool place, such as a root cellar.

&❧ The coarseness of the texture varies too, with some trees yielding fruits that feature tough gravel-like granules, prompting yet another epithet used for the pear: gravel pear.

&❧ However, any of these strange pears may be cooked or made into a jam or chutney that passes anyone's muster. They also yield a tart pear sauce and a pear cider richer in taste than the best that any apple can offer.

&❧ The tree, like all pear trees, is a slender, graceful oval, and the branches form a pattern that comes close to being symmetrical. It needs no spraying.

&❧ "When it comes to this kind of pear, the name doesn't mean anything," says Dr. Miklos Faust of the Horticulture Institute of the U.S. Department of Agriculture in Beltsville, Maryland. According to Faust, the so-called Maryland pear and the French quince pear are both descendants of pears that were once imported from China and were bred and crossbred with European pears. However, the precise genealogical lines of these pears can no longer be traced.

&❧ There are two great pear dynasties in the world. The first, originating in France, produced sweet pears that have the softness and the texture of butter, such as Bosc, Anjou, and Bartlett. The second dynasty, probably from China originally, offered tart pears with a hard, crisp texture that eventually turns slightly soupy.

&❧ European pears have that distinctively elongated pear shape that the French and the Italians have appreciated as esthetically pleasing. Far Eastern pears are rotund and look much like apples.

❧ In France and Italy, pear hybridization has been going on for centuries. The pear's status as a fruit of choice goes back at least as far as the Middle Ages and was often enhanced by royal favor. For instance, Louis XIV, France's Sun King, preferred pears to all other fruits, and he rewarded with gold pieces bearing his likeness all those gardeners and farmers who presented him with a new type of pear. In China, where pear breeding might well have been going on for thousands of years, the emphasis is on a hardy, vigorous tree that bears a large harvest.

❧ There is no native pear indigenous to the American continent, and the settlers brought in European varieties. But in the humid climate of the New World, many pear trees acquire a disease called fire blight, which makes the trees look as if their branches had been singed. The bacteria causing fire blight comes from related trees, such as mountain ash, hawthorn, pyracantha, and crab apple. Fire blight kills twigs and branches, and may eventually kill the tree.

❧ Two things can be done to prevent fireblight. One is to prune back the infested branches during winter. Make the cut eight to ten inches below the affected portion. Burn the wood that was cut off and treat the loppers in alcohol, because the fire blight bacteria spread easily. There are also sprays that can be applied, one of which is the antibiotic streptomycin.

❧ The other way to prevent fire blight is to plant varieties resistant to the disease. European pears in this country are susceptible to fire blight because their ancestors in Europe did not encounter it and thus did not develop immunity to it. But in China, which has a humid climate and where fire blight bacteria are present, hybridizers seem to have selected those pear trees that best resisted the disease. Or perhaps it was a case of natural selection.

❧ American botanists who went to China from the 1870s on found plenty of promising, disease-resistant, superior pear trees. Upon their return home, they started an extensive hybridization program. Because Americans preferred the taste of

European pears, the botanists focused on producing new varieties with the fire blight resistance of the Chinese trees but with the taste of the European pears. Those recommended these days are Seckel, Dawn, and Moonglow.

❧ One European pear with a superior taste that the Montgomery County Extension Service in Maryland warns against as particularly susceptible to fire blight is Clapp's Favorite.

❧ A few varieties retaining at least some of the taste of the Chinese pear were distributed by both orchardists and birds, particularly in the South, where fire blight is most widespread. But perhaps because the experimental station that worked on the Chinese pears is in Maryland, the state received more than a fair share of the stocks.

❧ Around the turn of the century, Oriental pear stocks were also brought in by immigrants from the Far East. Today those pears are well known in California, where they are called Asia pears or Japan pears.

❧ In Maryland and elsewhere on the Eastern Seaboard, there was yet another reason for the spread of Oriental pears: plants sprouted from seeds from pear cores tossed aside, and the ones that survived and grew into trees were usually those with the more vigorous Oriental genes in ascendance.

❧ Dr. Miklos Faust recommends Oriental pears wherever there is fire blight. "But," he adds, "you have to love the taste."

13
Magic Hawthorn

Throughout winter, the hawthorn's leafless boughs and twigs outlined against the sky are as articulated as a skeleton, and our eyes are as drawn to them as to the rich detail of a Dürer etching that fills every square inch with meaningful motion. The spring foliage is a lively, dense, glossy green, which in most varieties turns scarlet or orange in the fall. Then, most important, the sprays of hawthorn flowers come in white and pink, and, lately, in crimson and scarlet, and the red or orange berries that follow often last all winter long, all of them favored by birds and some of them edible to humans in the form of jams, preserves, and even liqueurs.

ба Moreover, hawthorn is the tree to plant if the soil is poor or heavy with clay. Seldom growing above the height of eighteen feet and accepting the discipline of shearing, the hawthorn is ideal for a small garden where a maple or an oak would be overwhelming.

ба Nevertheless, the hawthorn is an undervalued tree, seldom planted in the United States and praised even less frequently. One complaint focuses on its thorns, pointed and often formidable, which can make climbing and pruning risky. But the thorns are a useful feature when the objective is a

Hawthorn

screen to protect the garden from neighborhood cats, dogs, and other unwelcome intruders. With long, curved spines, the variety called Thicket Hawthorn can be sheared to produce an impenetrable screen or an effective hedgerow that is dense and shrubby, stays under the height of ten feet, and offers a snowstorm of white blooms. An even more showy choice as a barrier, and just as suitable for unresented shearing, is another native American hawthorn known as cockspur thorn (or haw), which is celebrated for its red flowers, bright red berries, and thick, twiggy growth. Both varieties offer a habitat for wildlife such as rabbits and foxes, and birds including grosbeaks and grouse.

&. A more serious objection to the hawthorn has to do with the controversial scent of its flowers, which has been called fishy and pestilential—and worse. In England, where the native hawthorn—also called thornapple, mayapple, whitethorn, and mayflower—is a sentimental favorite, it is seldom planted near the house, but usually some distance from it, most often to mark the boundaries of property.

&. But not all varieties have an unpleasant odor; in fact, most of the new and improved red-flowered hawthorns have either no odor or a pleasant, almondlike fragrance. It is best to ask the nursery about the scent of the hawthorns it grows and insist on an unscented variety.

&. Yet another impediment to greater popularity in the United States is that the hawthorn has a lingering reputation as an unlucky tree. From time immemorial, pagan lore in the Old World identified the hawthorn as a tree of magic powers. In his book *The White Goddess,* Robert Graves traces the hawthorn to the malevolent chief of the Welsh giants, Yspaddaden Penkawr, and derives its Celtic name, *sceith,* a cognate of the English "scathe," from the ominous word "harm." In its transformation as the death goddess, the Greek goddess Maia cast evil spells with branches of hawthorn blossoms. Graves wrote: "The Greeks propitiated her at marriages—marriage considered hateful to the goddess—with five torches of hawthorn wood and with hawthorn blossoms before the unlucky month began."

≥♣ However, the hawthorn is one of the trees celebrated in joyous festivals as the May Tree or May Pole, and one of its names is simply "may"—after the month it flowers. In medieval England, there was a custom of riding out to the countryside on May mornings to pluck hawthorn blooms and to dance around the maypole.

≥♣ In some cultures such as the Roman, the hawthorn's flowering period was associated with an abstention from sexual intercourse, including a ban on marriages, and in pagan England and Greece, it was thought to be most unlucky to wear new clothes until after the hawthorn blooms were spent. In Ireland, it is still considered exceedingly perilous to cut down a hawthorn tree, particularly an old one; and consequences are thought to include loss of one's vitality, children, cattle, and property.

≥♣ The "ascetic use of hawthorn" should be distinguished from its "later orgiastic use," Graves notes. He adds that for many men hawthorn blossoms have "a strong scent of female sexuality, which is why the Turks use a flowering branch as an erotic symbol."

≥♣ The hawthorn has also been venerated. One of England's most famous plants—and a place of pilgrimage—is the Glastonbury thorn, a hawthorn that according to Christian legend was originally a staff carried by Joseph of Arimathea who traveled to England from the Holy Land after the crucifixion of Jesus and built a Christian church in Glastonbury, which was then, as now, believed to be the island of Avalon, where King Arthur and Queen Guinevere are thought to have been buried. Joseph's staff took root and grew into a stately tree that bloomed on Christmas Day, as opposed to the common native hawthorn which blooms in May.

≥♣ Descendants of the tree, which botanists think was either a nonnative hawthorn or a genetic mutation, are still growing in the area around the ruins of Glastonbury Abbey, and their blooming time is still on or about Christmas Day.

🐝 However, according to Graves—a poet who was quick to expose what he suspected was a public relations stunt—the Glastonbury thorn's connection with the Holy Land was devised by the monks "as a means of discouraging the orgiastic use of hawthorn blossom."

🐝 Whether one's faith is pagan or Christian, monotheistic or pantheistic, it is hard not to be impressed with the elemental energy of the hawthorn. It is most appropriate that the botanists who named the hawthorn chose for it *Crataegus,* derived from the Greek word for "strength."

🐝 Hawthorn branches are sturdy and the twigs numerous, and they have a pattern and a balance that are picturesque. Wider than it is tall, the hawthorn is a spreading storybook tree, approximately symmetrical and frequently with a flat top when mature. Its many varieties offer a surprising diversity of leaf forms ranging from the plain toothed oval to the deeply lobed. Its flowers are invariably plentiful. One of the most floriferous varieties, called Paul's Scarlet, has double scarlet flowers so abundant that they render the branches invisible. A highly praised English hybrid—an heir of Paul's Scarlet and another old variety called Charles X—is aptly named Crimson Cloud; it has an airy abundance of single blooms that are bright red but with a star-shaped white area in the center. A cluster of the individual blooms forms a half-dome.

🐝 Unlike many other trees, hawthorns do not interfere with the growth of grass plants if planted in the midst of a lawn. Nor do the evils of urban pollution pose a problem for hawthorns. Another advantage is that they may be dug up and confidently replanted, even if many of their roots are cut off in the process.

🐝 Still more unusual is that all American hawthorns come true from seed. The seeds should first be freed from their pulp, or separated through soaking the berries in water. Then the seeds need to be kept moist in flats, stored in a cool cellar for as long as two years. Often germination does not take place until as late as the third spring, which is a long wait. But once a foot-long sapling is planted out, the gardener is entitled to have the confidence that the hawthorn will grow up fast, and live long and prosper, providing shade and beauty for several generations of humanity.

14
Under the Spreading Walnut Tree

If you are on the lookout for a large, substantial, storybook tree to provide deep shade and a reliable harvest of fruit year after year, and for several generations, a walnut tree should be at the top of your list.

&. But when you think of adding a walnut tree to your landscape, you should remember to plant more than one. For regular pollination, at least two trees are needed, and three is even more of a guarantee. They must be planted at least thirty feet away from the house and from other structures such as a garage or a swimming pool, and the trees ought to be at least forty feet from each other, because a walnut tree may eventually develop a spread of forty feet. Its height approaches a hundred feet. The best time to plant a walnut tree is in early spring or in midautumn, either prior to the hot weather that withers leaves or after the heat has petered out.

&. The walnut tree's sturdy branches bend and fork in such ways that they are easy to climb, and there is always a powerful horizontal bough perfect for a swing. However, if you have small children, or one is on the way, it is best to plant a walnut tree as soon as possible because the walnut is a slow grower and you want children clambering up the branches before they become teenagers in search of other forms of diversion.

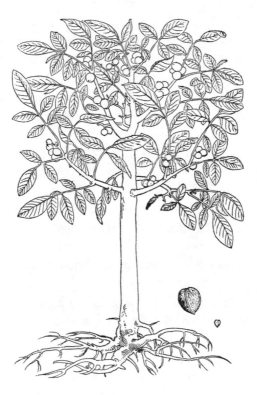

Walnut

❦ There are not many walnut trees growing in the United States, although they do well throughout the corn belt, and they could be grown in most parts of the country and in most soils. Some ninety percent of the U.S. supply of walnuts is from groves in California. The rest comes from Oregon.

❦ The native American walnut is known as the black walnut, once an important timber and food tree in the virgin forests of the Eastern Seaboard. Their stands are far fewer now, and the reasons for their reduction in number are unclear.

❦ Closely related to the black walnut is the Old World walnut, variously known as English, French, Persian, and Carpathian. A less-known native American walnut is the butternut, which is the hardiest member of the genus, doing well as far north as Maine.

❦ Though black walnuts are less plentiful and harder to pick and crack than the European walnut, their nutritional value is considerable. Today, black walnuts are recommended by experts, such as Mark Kantor of the University of Maryland, for being "an exceptionally good source of copper," an element that many scientists believe can help prevent heart disease. In addition, black walnuts contain lots of protein and some zinc, manganese, phosphorus, magnesium, and calcium.

❦ While black walnuts sometimes have a slightly bitter taste, European walnuts do not. Another difference is that the roots of the black walnut tree exude a toxic substance that kills or at least slows down the growth of most surrounding vegetation, particularly grass plants. European varieties are a bit more tolerant in allowing other plants to live in their shade.

❦ Most nurseries do not stock any walnut trees because there is little demand for them. Explaining the lack of popularity, nursery owners say people are reluctant to plant walnut trees because unlike other fruit trees, walnut trees do not have pretty blooms. Nor do they have great fall color or the kind of ornamental value many gardeners look for.

❦ But perhaps the strongest inhibiting factor is that grower satisfaction is delayed for too many years. It may take as long as seven years before a walnut tree bears a few token nuts, and another five before the tree really starts producing, filling sack after sack. Walnut trees are for people who are patient and who plan to stay put.

🍂 Unlike apples and pears, walnuts do not have nationally recognized top varieties, though nut-lovers do recommend Stabler, Ohio, and Thomas among the cultivated black walnut varieties, and Gebhart, Burtner, and Budman among the Europeans.

🍂 Walnut saplings are available through catalogs; often sold bare-rooted, they take root easily. But if you are lucky to find a grower, ask about the size of the nut, which can be anywhere between a Ping-Pong ball and a tennis ball. You will want a variety that promises large quantities of generously sized walnuts easy to crack. But if you find a grower who experiments, it is best to say, "Give me the finest you've got."

🍂 "The best walnuts are those you have never heard of," says Raymond Garst of Keymar, Maryland, who has been cultivating nut trees since 1979, which is very recent by walnut standards. What that means is that his trees are just beginning to take off and show how good they are.

🍂 Originally a dairy farmer and a cherry orchardist, Garst branched out, so to speak, by planting nut trees of various kinds. He has been busy cross-pollinating them in the hope of developing new and superior varieties, as well as new and unusual crosses such as one involving a European walnut, a heartnut, and a butternut.

🍂 He has also grafted scores of walnut trees, with the sturdy native black walnut usually serving as the rootstock. With a grafted tree, the grower knows the characteristics of the nut, which are the same as those of the scion's tree.

🍂 Garst prefers to sprout the nuts, which he finds exciting, even though he has to wait for many years before he knows what he has. He also complains that grafting nut trees is tricky. The temperature must be around seventy degrees to graft, he says, and you have to wait until the stock stops "bleeding." Otherwise, the graft won't take. And nut trees, like grapevines, bleed long and plenty.

❧ Garst has many rows of nut tree seedlings planted only a few inches apart. He started many of them from seed, which in this case simply means a nut, and all of the nuts came from trees that are outstanding producers. He charges for the saplings by the foot, and he digs up a customer's choices bare-rooted, with a powerful, eight-foot-long digging iron he fashioned out of pipes.

❧ Garst praises a Japanese walnut—which is sometimes called a heartnut because it is shaped like the human heart—that stands in his cousin's yard just outside Frederick, Maryland. The shells are thin and easy to crack, he says, and the meat tastes great.

❧ The nuts of another row for which he has high hopes come from a tree that grows on a friend's property. That tree offers a nut nearly the size of a tennis ball, has superior sweet taste, and its meat is easy to remove. As with the cousin's tree in Frederick, the friend's tree has no name by which it may be identified by botanists or in the nursery trade. Legend has it that it was planted about a century ago by an immigrant who brought a bagful of walnuts from the Old World, but no one remembers his place of origin.

❧ For people who have ailing old walnut trees, Garst recommends rejuvenating them instead of cutting them down. To perform the rejuvenation process, saw off all rotting limbs, he says, and spread fertilizer and lime all around, as far as the crown of the tree reaches. Every spring for several years, scatter bags of 10-10-10 fertilizer, one pound for every inch of the trunk's diameter. Use the same measurement for lime.

❧ Garst has a method for planting bare-rooted nut trees: Dig a large hole so all the roots can spread comfortably. The tip of the taproot, which may be snipped off if injured, should stand in a few inches of topsoil or improved soil. Tamp down the soil as you throw it on the roots, but do not use fertilizer or manure. Always use good garden soil. Once the tree stands, and the roots are buried and have solid contact with the soil, put dry, aged manure on the surface—but do not let it touch the trunk.

◆ It is critical, Garst says, that nut tree roots spread without interference from grass plants or weeds. Mulching the area around the trunk is best. Use anything that kills competition, such as grass clippings, straw, hay, or pine bark.

◆ Once properly established, a nut tree can grow as much as three feet a year, he says. Hybrids grow faster and start yielding fruit earlier than either parent did.

◆ Across the European continent, walnut trees are highly valued as a legacy left by thoughtful forebears. "A smart man had his grandfather plant walnut trees," is a common saying in Central Europe, where a walnut grove is a reliable source of prosperity and a pair of fine walnut trees suggests a solid, well-managed household.

◆ Growing up in the shade of an old walnut tree is an Old World metaphor for comfort, warmth, and tradition. Its foliage has a subtle scent that people like and flies and other insects do not. In my family, it is said that taking an afternoon nap under a spreading walnut tree inspires pleasant dreams—and those dreams may come true.

◆ Harvesting the nuts is a joyous chore, and storing them in a dry cellar or in boxes filled with sawdust ensures that not a nut goes to waste. On winter evenings, Mother brings a bowlful of walnuts in from the pantry, and Father or some uncle or cousin has a way of cracking two nuts together with bare hands and a seemingly effortless twist of the wrist. Every small piece of nut is carefully removed and eaten, and the shells, collected in another bowl, are tossed into the fire, where they light up with blue and green flames.

15
The Good Old Persimmon Tree

W hen driving on old country roads in late fall, we often pass by a stately tree that cannot be mistaken for any other: up to forty feet tall, with a slender brownish-gray trunk deeply furrowed and ramrod straight, it has nearly leafless, roughly symmetrical horizontal branches that are weighed down with masses of fruit, the color of ripe apricots and the size of Ping-Pong balls or a little smaller, and almost as round. The tree's name is persimmon, which comes from the Algonquin Indian word *pessemin*.

• It is a roadside tree gracing narrow back roads that have not been widened, and its fruits, dropping off ripe or nearly ripe from October on into winter, used to be snapped up by hungry travelers making their way on foot or on a horse. But these days motorists seldom stop and get out to sample a persimmon harvest, however inviting it looks as it carpets the ground and clearly to be had for free.

• Each fruit has a cluster of as many as six seeds in its center, and a seed may be as large as the largest pumpkin seed or as small as an apple seed. It germinates readily and grows into a tree that starts bearing fruit in five years. A roadside specimen is usually surrounded by a number of saplings that sprouted from seeds spat out or from a fruit that rotted on the ground.

European Date-plum

❧ A young persimmon tree is easy to dig up and to transplant in the fall or the spring. It will do well in poor soil, wet or dry, but it does insist on plenty of sun.

❧ There is also a closely related Oriental persimmon, which the Japanese call *kaki,* believed to have originated in China and also common in Korea. The tree has a shorter, bushier, symmetrical shape and a round fruit that can be as large as an orange, or as small as an Italian prune. Italians, Greeks, and the peoples of the Soviet Caucasus love the fruit and appreciate the tree and its hard and lustrous wood, which is used for making handles for tools.

❧ Both trees are highly ornamental, displaying dense canopies of glossy, oblong leaves of dark green that come out late in spring. In this country, the native persimmon fruit is seldom sold commercially, mostly because it does not travel well. The Oriental varieties are grown for sale mostly in California.

❧ The native American persimmon is one of the original fruits of the continent, appreciated for many centuries by American Indians who ate it raw, and also made a kind of bread out of it or mixed it in with meat. It is also a favorite of many kinds of birds, as well as raccoons, foxes, and possums. Even dogs eat it. The fruit is smooth-skinned, and from up close the color ranges from wan yellow to bright orange and pinkish red. The flavor is sweet, suggesting an apricot to some and a date to others, prompting the name "date plum." The texture is creamy. But the flavor is enjoyable only when the fruit is fully ripe, which means that it must be squishy-soft, but not yet fermented. Fermentation can begin within twenty-four hours if the weather turns warm.

❧ When unripe, American persimmons are what botanists call astringent, and others dismiss as puckery; they constrict lips, tongue, and throat, and they have an aftertaste suggesting a wet woolen blanket.

❧ Most Oriental persimmons have been selected and bred

to be free of any astringency. But for the best sweet-and-sour flavor, it is a good idea to wait until they too are squishy-soft.

❧ Unripe persimmons, American or Oriental, ripen faster when placed in a plastic bag along with a slice of apple or banana and closed airtight. When left at room temperature for three days or more, the apple or banana will release a gas that will naturally speed up the process of ripening, which would otherwise take two weeks.

❧ The American persimmon tree is sold by Burpee and some small nurseries that specialize in native and wild plants. Unlike the cultivated Oriental persimmon tree, which must be protected from the north wind, the native needs no coddling.

❧ Whichever kind of persimmon tree you plant, it is best to choose a site that is sunny and well drained. Persimmon trees need no fertilizers, and some experts even argue against watering them the way other trees are watered in the fall. Anything that encourages late growth is unhealthy for the persimmon tree because the tender new growth is likely to be killed by a hard freeze.

❧ As it grows vertically, the native persimmon tree loses its lowest horizontal branches, and it is not uncommon to see a trunk free of side growth for twelve feet off the ground. Such a structure is just right for a mixed border of sun-loving flowers underneath.

16
The Pear Trees of Bethesda

Spring is the time to praise the pear trees of Bethesda, Maryland. Their mantles of white blossoms may be gone after as brief a spell as one week, but for the rest of the year, the elegant ovals formed by their symmetrical branches will redeem many miles of asphalt wilderness, for instance the median strip of busy Wisconsin Avenue between Western Avenue and East-West Highway.

෴ They are tidy, densely branched, robust trees that line up as if they were drawn by an artist illustrating a nineteenth-century novel of romance. When they bloom—a period that lasts two weeks at best, if there is no rain and the weather does not turn warm—they look as insubstantial as if they were conjured up by Shakespeare's Prospero on his magic island.

෴ Poets and painters have immortalized the great spreading horse chestnut trees of boulevards in Paris and Vienna, and the carefully sheared lindens of Berlin allées. And of course Americans across the nation join in to celebrate the extravaganza of the blooming cherry trees of Washington, D.C.

෴ However, I know of no poem or novella or civic festival that would have put on the map the pear trees of Bethesda. They have no national or international fame, and thus far they have not become metaphors for anything.

➷ The pear trees that form those fine allées on many streets in Bethesda and adorn countless front and back yards elsewhere in the country belong to a species of ornamental pear called Callery pear, which is a native of eastern China. The cultivar is known as Bradford Pear. The trees bear a minuscule, inedible fruit or nothing at all. What makes the Bradford Pear special is its delicate white blossom, which breaks out in early spring as soon as there is a week of sixty-degree weather.

➷ The blossoms come in a hard-to-believe abundance. From a distance, it appears as if a blizzard left the tree covered with a thick blanket of snow. From close up, one is struck by the layers of immaculate petals, which are symmetrically clustered and so dense that they render branches and leaves invisible.

➷ Once the blooms are gone, the vigorous, upright, evenly spaced branches with their masses of glossy green leaves are pleasing to the eye throughout spring and summer. But the finest moment of the foliage is late fall, when the leaves turn a brilliant crimson.

➷ The Bradford Pear is one of the most popular flowering trees not only in the Washington metropolitan area but across the country as well. It was selected some three decades ago at the Glenn Dale Maryland Station of the U.S. Department of Agriculture out of its collection of thousands of pear trees. They are ornamental, which means that they specialize in pretty blooms rather than edible fruits.

➷ Many of the trees were grown from more than a hundred pounds of seeds collected in China in the first years of the century by the famous American botanist and plant collector Frank Meyer, who roamed the forests and parks of the Middle Kingdom. Other seeds, including Bradford's, were purchased from the Chinese in 1919. Though for centuries China was famous for the beauty of its ornamental pears—as well as cherries and plums—no Chinese plantsman is known to have been responsible for selection and hybridization. It appears that the different varieties developed by natural selection, and aficionados searched the countryside for the finest specimen

❧ At various experimental stations of USDA, botanists first select the trees with the most desirable characteristics, such as resistance to pests and diseases, good shape, strong branch structure, largeness and beauty of bloom, and then cross them in the hope that at least one of the offspring will inherit all the desirable characteristics and none of the undesirable ones, such as vulnerability to diseases and weaknesses in structure and shape.

❧ Bradford was identified as a superior plant in 1963 and named after F. C. Bradford, USDA horticulturist. The tree was then propagated vegetatively—cloned from branches—and the offshoots were sent out to take root across the country.

❧ The Bradford Pear is remarkably resistant to disease and pollution. It does not mind emissions from automobile exhaust pipes, and it thrives in gardens with the minimum of care or even no care at all. It needs no sprays. It grows up to thirty-five feet in height, but unless its lower forks were properly pruned in its youth, its limbs may eventually become brittle and split in high winds.

❧ Those planted on Bethesda's streets in the 1960s are reaching their old age and some of them have been removed already. Their replacement is not Bradford but another variety called Whitehouse, which was developed at the National Arboretum where specialists are convinced that it is the new superior ornamental pear tree. Named after a botanist, not the famous Washington building, Whitehouse is more slender in shape than Bradford, but with a stronger, heftier trunk and branches that are much less likely to splinter and snap. Gardeners who have grown both say that in the fall Whitehouse turns color a little earlier than Bradford and has an even more spectacular display of leaves, ranging from scarlet to deep purple.

❧ Similar to Whitehouse and selected from the same genetic pool is another new superior variety called Capitol, which has been singled out for its columnar shape and narrow, pyramidal crown, which is convenient for tight spaces. It flowers early, and its foliage turns crimson in the early fall. A pair of them on either side of an entranceway dresses up a front yard.

❧ The Aristocrat is another recently developed narrow ornamental pear, with a dense branching habit. Still another competitor on tough city streets is Redspire; its flowers are larger than Bradford's, and in the fall its foliage turns a shade between crimson and purple.

❧ For those who do not have the space or prefer a smaller tree, a variety called Faurei is a fine dwarf ornamental pear. It does not grow taller than twenty-five feet, and in the fall its foliage turns orange, crimson, and purple. Faurei has all the symmetries and the compact growth habits of its tall cousins.

❧ For those who find the ornamental cherry gaudy or complain about the far too prolific and unruly branches of crab apple trees, the ornamental pear is an elegant, unproblematic alternative. Whether oval Whitehouse, columnar Capitol, or dwarf Faurei, the state-of-the-art ornamental pear is a flowering tree that dazzles us with its colors in spring and fall, and pleases us with its symmetries during summer and winter.

17
Second Chance for Apple Trees

Resist the temptation for a radical solution if the property you have just bought includes a crazy, overgrown apple tree that looks like a vertical brush pile.

🙠 Old apple trees should be rescued—saved from the consequences of their own exuberance. They can be rejuvenated and live over a hundred years. A restored apple tree that mixes old, weathered branches with fresh, smooth growth is as unique as a settler's log cabin that has been patched with new wood.

🙠 Whether neglected or carefully trained, an old apple tree has character that comes from its branches having forked and thrust out in many directions over the years. It looks as if no part of an apple tree can grow in a straight line for more than a few inches at a time—nor can it keep itself from branching off. Whatever framework the main limbs develop is routinely subverted by abrupt downward thrusts of branches and by tangles of crossing twigs. In contrast to the pear tree—a close relative—which is tidy and the fairly symmetrical branches of which bend gently in growing upright, the apple tree is a restless, ragged clutter of acute and obtuse angles. More so than other fruit trees, the apple tree cries out for the gardener's pruning saw and lopping shears.

Apple

❧ A crisp winter day—any day after the leaves fall—is the ideal time for pruning back live branches, vigorous or puny. However, cutting off dead and diseased branches may be done at any time, in fact as soon as their condition is diagnosed.

❧ Pruning cuts should be made in such a way that no stubs remain after the cut is completed—only a "collar," much like a shirt collar, an inch or so wide. Healing proceeds quickly on properly made cuts, but a stub will prevent the cut from healing.

❧ Experts now recommend that the wound be left undressed and that the tree should be left to its own considerable devices to isolate the cut and prevent rotting and the entrance of harmful organisms. If you feel compelled to apply a dressing or a paint you have had in the shed for years, at least avoid using materials that contain creosote. Creosote has been identified as a cancer-causing substance.

❧ An important project, best to be undertaken in the fall, is to eliminate all suckers. They are stems, usually extremely vigorous, which emerge from the rootstock. Each sucker has to be pulled off by hand, along with its base. If you cut them off neatly with pruning shears, you will leave a cluster of dormant buds at the base, which may then later grow into multiple suckers resembling a broom. Brutal yanking by hand does the job better, and you need not feel guilty about it.

❧ The water sprout is another type of unwanted growth. Sometimes also called a sucker, the water sprout is often an extraordinarily vigorous stem that tends to shoot up vertically in one season, usually parallel with the main trunk and unmistakably in competition with it. Water sprouts should be cut off flush, and the sooner the better.

❧ Both suckers and water sprouts divert a great deal of energy from the main limbs of the tree. They are rebels who in one quick burst of energy want to take over from the slowly growing, established framework of limbs.

❧ A long-neglected, overgrown old apple tree should be rejuvenated over two to four years, in stages. Starting with a reduction of the height of a tree is sound strategy, and there is nothing wrong with removing at once two or even three large limbs that go out too far or cross one another. (The best time for major surgery is winter when the tree is dormant, and it may be said "to feel no pain.") New limbs will take the places of the old, and they may be trained with wire in order for them to spread in the right directions and to develop those wide angles that make for a sturdier, healthier framework.

🍂 Experts suggest clearing the center of the tree's foliage to let more sunshine in and to encourage better air circulation. Overcrowding is not good for the tree—neither for the blossoms nor for the fruits.

🍂 On the other hand, if the apple tree has one sturdy, sound upright trunk, it may be best to encourage a pyramidlike structure by removing the heftiest side branches.

🍂 Except during winter, cutting a tree back drastically at any one time is too much of a shock for the tree. Severe pruning also encourages a proliferation of water sprouts, which sap the tree's strength at a time when it is already under stress, and which must be removed, preferably as soon as they emerge.

🍂 If you do not have an apple tree and you are starting out in a new yard, it is a good idea to buy one—or, better yet, two. Age-old tradition believes in the wisdom of planting fruit trees in twos. The primary reason is cross-pollination; another, never mentioned by farmers but singled out by poets and other myth-makers, is that a pair of trees presents as inspiring a sight as a happily married couple.

🍂 Planting should be done in the fall or early spring, but a hefty, container-grown or balled-and-burlapped apple tree may be planted even during the summer, as long as the sky is overcast and the temperature is expected to stay under eighty degrees for the next three days.

🍂 The so-called spur-type apple tree offers more dense growth instead of far-spreading branches. Though a spreading apple tree has its appeal as a storybook tree, the compact spur-type is more suitable for the city garden.

&. Those who are considering planting a fruit tree should know that the apple is the number-one tree fruit in the temperate regions of the world. An apple tree requires a well-watered summer of at least one hundred consecutive days without frost and a winter dormancy of at least one thousand hours between forty-five degrees above zero and thirty degrees below.

&. As for apple blooms, they are supernally white and come out in delicate sprays, forming a favorite subject of the Orient's traditional painters. Watching the fruits thicken and color is yet another source of satisfaction.

&. For most of the United States, the apple tree is the right tree to plant—and to preserve.

18
Cherry Glory

You know that your cherry tree has entered middle age when it is frequently visited by woodpeckers that hop up and down and sideways on the trunk and its branches. However, the cherry tree has reached a perilous state of senility when instead of the familiar busy woodpecker with a red spot on its head and the size of a starling, the visitor is the imposing pileated woodpecker—a dramatic black-and-white bird with lots of red in its plumage and the size of a large crow.

❧ The ordinary or downy woodpecker feeds on small insects and worms, often catching them inside the bark by punching small holes with its beak, with hammerblows faster and more persistent than the human hand is capable of. The pileated woodpecker is interested only in trees that have substantial chunks of seriously decaying or dead wood; in search of its food it will hit the wood slowly and methodically, and after repeated visits, it will eventually carve out a cavity spacious enough for a raccoon family residence.

❧ Sometimes the deterioration of the wood is exposed as the result of repeated initial probes by woodpeckers or by other animals burrowing into the softened, rotting texture. Sometimes

Cherry

the decaying or dead wood comes into plain view only after a branch weakened by borers breaks off in a storm, which happens often with cherry trees.

❧ Fortunately, the decline of cherry trees is reversible. That is particularly true in case of the ornamental cherry trees such as the early flowering, white-to-pink Yoshino of Washington, D.C.'s world-famous Tidal Basin and the two other Japanese varieties that bloom later and over a longer period of time: the pink double-flowering Kwanzan and the white Shirofugen. Yet another outstanding variety is the Weeping Higan, which in Washington and many other parts of the country is one of the earliest trees to flower, producing pale pink blossoms cascading from an abundance of long, drooping branches.

❧ These four trees—along with the April-blooming white Mount Fuji with a horizontal growth habit and the pinkish-white, fall-blooming Autumnalis—have made Washington the flowering cherry capital of the United States. (They do produce fruits too, but they are not enjoyable.) In many older neighborhoods, these trees have passed the age of fifty, which is close to the human equivalent of one hundred years. Unfortunately, some homeowners have given up and paid many hundreds of dollars to cut down their decaying cherry trees—instead of having them pruned.

❧ The best time for rescuing old cherry trees of all types is in early spring, after the wood and the bark are no longer brittle on account of the frost, and before the sap starts flowing again. The strategy is simple: saw off the decayed trunk or branch at a point where the wood is still firm and healthy, even if that means cutting a twenty-five-foot-tall trunk down to six feet. The odds are better than even for new and vigorous shoots to emerge near the cut, or from the base, or possibly at both points.

❧ The new growth may even be too vigorous, with tufts of whips suddenly bursting forth and racing to reach a length of more than a foot in one year. It is a good idea to keep in a tuft only the strongest whip, or the one that grows in the most desirable direction. Such a whip can be relied upon to turn into a thick branch in a few years. The rejuvenated tree may have an odd, intriguing structure: strongly asymmetrical, even out of balance. It will suggest a traditional Japanese painting.

🍃 Specialists in the National Arboretum advise against the use of any wax or paint to seal the sawed-off portion. Moreover, the technique nowadays recommended by the Arboretum for cutting off side branches is to leave a small "collar"—rather than to have a cut flush with the trunk, which is a mistake cited in many books on pruning. In the experience of the Arboretum—which deals with thousands of trees—a tree's wound heals better without a sealant but with a "collar" left intact.

🍃 Cherry trees may also be pruned in early spring, right after they flower, or in late summer or early fall, after they fruit. But for certain rejuvenation, the safest time for drastic pruning is during the dormant state.

🍃 One reason cherry trees respond to pruning so well is that their roots are exceptionally vigorous. If suddenly the roots no longer have the foliage they have been accustomed to support, they seem to demand replacement. It is not recommended that one prune a young cherry tree too enthusiastically because the result is lots of shoots, often in tufts and out of proportion with the rest of the structure. Removing lower branches, on the other hand, is a good idea—so one can walk under the tree—and the canopy will be more dense as a result, again because the roots try to compensate for the loss above.

🍃 Cherry branches cross and injure one another all the time, and a tree does not have to be old to produce a lot of puny and dead twigs. All such branches and twigs should be removed as soon as they are noticed.

🍃 The cherry tree is the strongest, hardiest, most persistent member of the distinguished genus Prunus, which includes trees both lovely and useful, such as almonds, peaches, apricots, nectarines, and plums. Whether ornamental or edible—whether its principal virtue is the blossom or the fruit—the cherry tree is the one that is likeliest to come back, even from a stump.

19
Champion Poplars

Y ou have just moved into a fine new house, but the property that surrounds it is a seamless expanse of grass, and there are no fences or screens to be seen anywhere in the development. The neighbors are nice, and putting up a fence may seem to them like an unfriendly act. But you really dislike the "commons" look and feel.

&. One way to liven up the emptiness around the house and gain some privacy without alienating the neighbors is to plant trees and locate them strategically and esthetically along the property lines. There are dozens of attractive possibilities, such as ornamental pear and cherry trees, which are deciduous—they lose their leaves during winter—or Leyland cypresses and Eastern white pine, which are reliably evergreen. But if you are really impatient, the deciduous hybrid poplar might just be the right plant for you.

&. A result of crossing a number of different Japanese (*Populus maximowiczii*) and Canadian (*Populus trichocarpa*) poplars, these fairly recent varieties are known collectively as "hybrid poplars," and they grow into symmetrical and virtually identical trees with a height that can easily measure an amazing forty feet within five years. They may well be the world's fastest growing trees, and at least in the temperate region they are the

Poplar

unquestioned champions. They are advertised as the perfect instant solution for allées and screens as visual and sonic barriers, and for covering any site, including severely disturbed ones. In addition, hybrid poplars are marketed as representing a reliably bountiful source of firewood.

❧ Nevertheless, most horticultural experts do not recommend hybrid poplars for the ornamental garden. They point out that poplars lack flowers and lovely autumn color, and that their leaves tend to look coarse. In brief, hybrid poplars are not ornamental enough, though they are perhaps acceptable as barriers and useful (and profitable) on a farm as a pulpwood crop. The experts further warn that with many poplars, such as the tall and narrow Lombardy poplar, there are additional problems: suckers keep coming up persistently, the roots' unquenchable thirst poses a threat to water-carrying pipes and even to septic systems, and, last but not least, the branches snap easily in windstorms. The best hybrid poplars are not as dangerous, the experts add, but fast-growing trees in general do not spend sufficient time and energy to develop strong, dense fibers, and such trees do not live long. Indeed, even a good hybrid poplar's maximum lifetime of thirty to forty years does not measure up to a run-of-the-mill oak's one hundred years plus.

❧ Hybrid poplars originally came from experimental stations, which keep seeking vigorous, fast-growing trees to provide pulp wood and to reforest sanitary landfills, strip mines, and other wastelands created in the name of progress and prosperity. In the early 1950s, the Northeastern Forest Experiment Station produced some of the first hybrid poplars in the country and offered them, eight cuttings for one dollar, to anyone willing to plant them and then report back on how they fared.

❧ Miles Fry, a dairy farmer from Ephrata, Pennsylvania, was among those who responded. All eight of his unrooted cuttings, each some ten inches long, took root in March and grew to an unbelievable height of ten feet by October. They were healthy, ramrod straight, and nice to look at. Then a most unexpected thing happened: in place of each of the rods he cut off as an experiment, another rod grew to the same size in the same period of time as the original cutting. Soon, he was selling the rods, which were of uniform thickness and flexibility, to mines, and he was also selling rooted hybrid poplars as shade trees and landscape screens. After the Arab oil embargo of 1973, the Fry farm branched out into the enterprise of converting chopped-up hybrid poplar chips into ethyl alcohol, which cost them about $1.15 per gallon.

&. In 1982, Miles Fry died, and his son Morton took over the family business. Now in his early sixties, Morton Fry sounds like an angry prophet. He argues that because of the relatively low energy prices, the dream of energy independence, which ought to be a national goal, is not being realized. The energy market focuses on short-range interests, he says. The nation has a total of up to 500 million acres of marginal and abandoned farmland, he says, citing data from the U.S. Department of Agriculture, and such lands are ideal for growing hybrid poplars. Because of their speedy growth, it is possible to produce 59.8 million BTUs per acre per year. The only other trees that even come close to such a figure are cottonwood (also a poplar) and mulberry, but neither lends itself to farmlike cultivation. Planting hybrid poplars should be a national priority, he says.

&. While Mort Fry continues to hybridize poplars, he sells by the tens of thousands three varieties developed by others. The smooth-barked and densely-leaved Androscoggin Poplar is for the shade. For screens of all types, his recommendation is the Red Caudina—so named because of the red veins in its leaves—which has short limbs in large numbers, giving a narrow form at maturity. For both shade and screen, he offers *Charkowiensis incrassata*. It has a columnar habit as well as reddish veins in its leaves.

&. Mort Fry rejects the criticisms of botanists. "There is no down side to my best hybrid poplars," he says. "They take wind and ice, and they don't break. They are not like Lombardy poplars." He concedes that they should not be planted near a septic plant or even drain fields. All poplars have aggressive root systems, so they should be planted at least thirty feet from water-carrying pipes. As for their suckering habit, the hybrids he has developed do not have it, he says. There is no comparable tree that can cover huge piles of refuse or shale, or scarred and eroded land, he sums up, and botanists agree.

ᨑ As for the observation that hybrid poplars are short-lived, his response is that he would like to see "more longevity in our hybrid poplars. We are now looking at other poplars elsewhere in the world. We will have even better hybrids, and soon." It is good to hear him declare, in the authentic rural accent of Pennsylvania: "The future depends on geneticists rather than nuclear physicists."

ᨑ The Fry family has been restricting itself to poplars, Mort Fry says. "We have dedicated our lives to the poplar, and our family has the tenacity that is needed." And perhaps the most reassuring thing about the Fry search for a truly superior hybrid poplar is that his grandchildren are the ninth generation of Frys living on the same family farm.

20
The American Chestnut: Once and Future King?

Hiking in the Shenandoah Valley or through the mountains of West Virginia, one comes across a strange sight which, depending on the onlooker, either inspires or depresses: lively young stems rise out of a sprawl of massive, blackened stumps that look like burnt-out ruins.

🍂 The stumps are what is left of the American chestnut tree that once grew more than one hundred feet tall, with trunks sometimes reaching ten feet in diameter. For an uncounted number of centuries, those giants covered about one-fourth of the Appalachian forest, from Maine to the Gulf Coast, and as far west as the Mississippi River.

🍂 However, unlike the sprouts that launch a new incarnation of an upturned old apple tree, the chestnut branches are doomed. Within five years—usually before they have a chance to flower and set fruit—all the fresh growth withers and dies. Leaf and stem alike are killed by a mysterious bark fungus, the spores of which are carried across the country by the wind.

🍂 But one part of the tree left unaffected is the roots, which are vigorous and which keep sending out new shoots.

🍂 The lethal fungus, *Endothia parasitica,* is believed to have slipped into the New World in the first years of our century

Sweet or Spanish Chestnut

unobserved, along with some seedlings of the shorter, bushier Chinese chestnut, which were imported from China, like many other plants, for improving native stock. The fungus spread, and while it was ignored by the Chinese chestnut tree which had developed resistance to it through what might have been thousands of years, the American variety was defenseless. By the 1950s, some 30 million American chestnut trees were struck by the fungus.

🍂 Is the great American chestnut, once the king of the eastern hardwood forest, truly dead, never to return?

🍂 Acclaimed by botanists and woodworkers as the finest timber tree in the American forest, the American chestnut was the wood of choice for log cabins—spiders were said to stay away from it—as well as for fine-grained, top-of-the-line furniture, rot-resistant fence posts and fancy moldings. It did not splinter or warp, it did not decay, and its grain was as good as that of walnut.

🍂 "If you can't tell whether an old piece of wood is pine or oak, the chances are that it is chestnut," says David Johnson, a carpenter from Barnesville, Maryland, and a connoisseur of fine wood. "The American chestnut is a little too soft for oak and much too hard for pine, and it has a finer grain than either. For God's sake, don't throw away an old plank of chestnut just because it looks junky."

🍂 The Chinese chestnut tree does not have fine wood comparable to that of the American chestnut. But the Chinese variety is a lovely ornamental tree with a broad crown. It grows fast and may eventually reach a height of fifty feet, providing shade and tasty nuts.

🍂 Numerous attempts have been made to recover the glory of the American chestnut. For many years, the U.S. Department of Agriculture tried to produce a blight-resistant hybrid out of Chinese, Japanese, and American varieties. But the program, which was discontinued some twenty years ago, did not yield a hybrid resistant to the blight and one which would have provided timber comparable to that of the American chestnut. Nor were any of the hundreds of hybrids created comparable to the American chestnut as a forest tree.

❧ There is now a group dedicated to its revival, the American Chestnut Foundation, with Nobel Laureate Norman Borlaug as its founding director. One promising recent development is the discovery, in Europe, of a rival fungus that tends to "convert" the lethal chestnut fungus into an almost innocuous one. Though more research is needed, it seems now that once the "benign" fungus invades a chestnut tree, the lethal fungus stops killing the wood.

❧ A traditional approach has been followed for nearly forty years by Robert Dunstan, a plant breeder originally from Greensboro, North Carolina, and now retired in Alachua, Florida. In the early 1950s, Dunstan was given budwood from one of the few American chestnut trees that resisted the blight. He grafted the scions onto Japanese rootstock, and cross-pollinated the result with the Chinese varieties developed by the U.S. Department of Agriculture. Then he crossed back the offspring to the parent trees.

❧ Out of all this cross-breeding, he has developed a hybrid which he says has the tall, upright form of the American tree and the big production of the Chinese. Moreover, he adds, the Dunstan hybrids are large: 23 nuts to the pound is the record, which is excellent compared to the 75–150 for the American and 30–40 for the Chinese.

❧ "The best of our hybrids resemble the American chestnut most," says Robert Wallace, Dunstan's grandson, who manages Chestnut Hill Nursery, founded by Dunstan. "But, most important, not a single one of our hybrids has shown any evidence of being affected by the blight."

❧ Perhaps by the end of this century we will know if we can expect a return of the king.

The Triumph
of Evergreens

21
Ever Green, Ever Dear

T hank God for evergreens.

🍂 Whether their colors are emphatically verdant, or resplendent in tints of blue and silver, or dissolving in a golden haze, evergreens stand up against the coldest winter. Though robust in branch structure, they have a lighthearted grace, and the tracery of their foliage is invariably intricate.

🍂 During spring and summer, evergreen colors appear pallid, ever tired, when compared to the tender, fresh growth of oaks and maples, birches and beeches. Evergreens are at their most dramatic when half buried in snow and limned by crystals of ice. Their tips fairly shout for attention, as contours of the snowdrift adumbrate the arrangements of the branches underneath.

🍂 From a botanical point of view, evergreens are plants that keep their foliage and their colors through subzero temperatures even though they too go dormant like the trees that lose their leaves, and they are divided into two large categories: broad-leaved and narrow-leaved. While the former have flat leaves shaped in a variety of ways, the latter have foliage that resembles needles, and they are often bracketed in the vernacular as "Christmas trees." They are also called conifers (Latin: "cone-bearing") because of their cones—brownish, candlelike structures that contain seeds, in fact the earliest seeds of plant evolution.

❧ For the homeowner, there are hundreds of different evergreens to choose from, and the abundance of genera and their varieties is bewildering. One way to narrow down the choice is to define first the specific reason for which an evergreen is needed.

❧ One objective that makes a lot of sense is a high density of solid color, which may be formed by a hedge or a windbreak, or by just one plant, or by a pair of trees standing by the driveway or near the entrance to the house. For such a purpose, the American arborvitae is a traditional favorite, even though it lost some popularity in the past few decades, most probably because of its ubiquity. Nevertheless, if you want a steady, reliable, healthy splash of lively winter color, it is hard to find something better than the good old arborvitae.

❧ Its height can go up to sixty feet, but most of them grow only an inch or two a year once they reach twenty feet. Fertile, well-drained soil is preferred, but not required. Typically, the foliage is neat and symmetrical, and shaping with shears is rarely necessary. If pruning is needed, late winter is the best time for it.

❧ However, it is easier to buy an arborvitae variety in the size and shape desired and then leave it alone. For instance, if you want tall and pyramidal, choose a fast-growing variety called Douglas Pyramidal, which has been around for more than a century. Among low and compact varieties, the slow-growing Booth Globe is broader than tall, and roughly globe-shaped when mature. Hetz Junior is a round dwarf not going beyond the height of five feet. Increasingly popular is the Rheingold, seldom taller than ten feet, and with a golden foliage.

❧ For gardeners who want massive, dense growth but prefer free form to symmetry, the yew is a traditional alternative that seems to be staging a comeback in popularity. Whether in sun or shade, the yew is not a fast grower, but it will live for centuries. The short, stubby needles surrounding the supple twigs suggest a bottlebrush, and its branching habit may be characterized as frequently rambunctious, even if the variety was bred for a symmetrical shape.

🍂 Winter is the best time to prune a yew, and it does not stop growing even if severely pruned back. It is ideal for sculpting any desired shape, such as a swan or an archway. An old, overgrown yew may be cut back to the trunk without any fear of ruining it, and new growth will sprout out even from bare wood.

🍂 From prostrate shrubs to sixty-foot trees, from narrow columns to squat, wide-spreading multitrunked forms, there are dozens of yew varieties under each category such as English, Canadian, and Japanese. The ideal way to choose among them is to see their mature specimens in arboretums or to shop around in nurseries that carry a large variety of them.

🍂 For those who prefer loose, fluffy foliage to high density of color, the eastern white pine is an excellent choice. Known variously as white pine, Weymouth pine, and soft pine, the native *Pinus strobus* grows in the wild from Maine to Georgia and as far west as Minnesota, forming forests and growing in open meadows, and planted on slopes adjacent to highways as well as throughout new housing developments. It is the fastest-growing and least expensive evergreen tree, easy to recognize by its clusters of five slender, vividly blue-green needles up to five inches long. Its bark is gray and deeply fissured into broad ridges. Its cones are long and narrow, up to eight inches in length and yellowish brown in color.

🍂 When young, a white pine grows upright in a fairly symmetrical manner, but it gradually loses its symmetry with age. A youthful, pyramid-shaped white pine often acquires a flat top in twenty years, and its layers of branches eventually produce an arrangement that recalls a delicately balanced Japanese image, rather than a symmetrical Christmas tree.

❧ As the tree matures, it usually loses its lower branches. Unlike most other conifers, the white pine does not grow new branches where dead ones are cut off.

❧ It is not unusual for a well-established, mature white pine in a nice sunny location to add three to four feet of height a year, to a maximum of one hundred feet. Once it reaches fifteen feet, it is broad and airy, with plenty of space between its branches. It is a structure that some people admire as free and easy, but it also gives rise to a grumble: white pine takes up much too much room, and it is too fluffy for a privacy fence or a windscreen. In short, it is a puffy job, a tree of little substance. Careful pruning, to be done in the spring and in the first few years of the tree's life, can make the white pine more dense and give it a better shape.

❧ No list of evergreens is complete without a mention of the Leyland cypress, a nursery best-seller in the past ten years or so. It is a soft-edged tree, with a dense, lacy foliage in a faded, almost antique shade of green. Resistant to insects and diseases, the Leyland cypress has overtaken in popularity the American arborvitae, once the standard-bearer of evergreens in the home garden, as well as the yew, which used to be the number-one heavy-duty, all-purpose evergreen in public and private spaces. Unlike the arborvitae, the Leyland cypress is a fast grower, and its foliage does not turn brown, which is often the case with some of the older varieties of arborvitae.

❧ Standing alone as a specimen tree, both the white pine and the Leyland cypress seem to lack authority. They look their best when forming a stand with others of their kind.

❧ As a living fence, an evenly spaced row of white pine has a natural yet tidy appearance. For a spacious garden, white pines planted fifteen to twenty feet apart offer an attractive visual barrier.

❧ A closely spaced row—three to five feet—of Leyland cypress suggests cultivation and refinement. At the same time, it is also a fine privacy fence and windscreen. Cypresses may be pruned at any time, and their side branches will become more dense if the leader—the strong central stem—is cut back.

❧ Looking more substantial than the cypress is the hemlock. The Canada or Eastern hemlock (*Tsuga canadensis*) is a fast grower, particularly when treated with fertilizers. If fed with nitrogen, a healthy five-foot-tall Canada hemlock can add up to three feet of vertical growth in a year.

❧ The Canada hemlock requires good soil and ample moisture. Under such conditions, it grows like a weed, develops a graceful form, and offers a rich, strong green color. It keeps its lower branches for many years, but once the lower branches are gone, the reddish trunk provides what evergreen enthusiasts call "plenty of character."

❧ With thick, blunt needles half an inch long and a dense, roughly symmetrical branching habit, Canada hemlock has a robust presence in the yard as a single, so-called specimen tree. It is also good material for a hedge, provided that it is pruned lightly in the first few years as the plants establish their framework and fill out. A hemlock hedge needs to be pruned once a year, in early summer.

❧ Evergreens nowadays come in many shades of blue and gold as well as green, and undertones of bronze and even purple have been added to the palette. Most of these tints are now available in pine and cedar, yew and juniper. The time is approaching when a homeowner can choose a color first and then shop around for a genus.

❧ Choosing trees for their distinctive bark is a fairly recent preference, which is no longer restricted to connoisseurs. One of the most dramatic examples is the lace-bark pine, once a favorite of Chinese gardeners and scholars, but now widely planted across Europe as well as North America. The needles come in bundles, and there may be as many as half a dozen trunks, bent and twisted, leaning this way and that, and forking off frequently. The bark of the young branches is medium green, with splashes and streaks of brown and almost-white turning an occasional shade of cinnamon. As the years pass, the bark starts exfoliating, revealing plates of creamy-colored bark underneath.

❧ Given full sun and plenty of moisture, the lace-bark pine's eventual height is fifty feet.

❧ Less frequently grown in the United States is the Japanese cedar. Leafy and bushy when mature and often reaching a height of seventy feet, its bark is a brownish red tending toward cinnamon when it starts to peel.

❧ In the dead whiteness of winter, evergreens are here to remind us that spring must be on its way. Rising up from under the snow, a hedgerow of yew or the spire of an arborvitae reassures us with their color.

22
Homage to the King of the Forest

There are two kinds of Christmas trees for Elvira Brandt Hanna. There is a third as well, which she thinks is superior to the other two, but she is not quite sure if it is all right to call that a proper Christmas tree.

  🍂 Hanna is a Washingtonian who grew up in Germany, which is the country of origin for the now worldwide tradition of celebrating the Christmas season with a decorated conifer—an evergreen tree bearing cones. She remembers that in the Germany of her childhood, the popular tree was either a Norway spruce or an Austrian pine—the two fine conifers most common in the mountains of Central and Northern Europe. Before World War II, they were the Christmas trees that Germans either bought in the marketplace or cut down in the forests then covering much of their country. They looked for a strong, symmetrical structure, plenty of straight, hefty side branches, and an absolute abundance of densely packed needles. The overall color had to be dark, dark green—a green as dark as the snow was white. This was the first kind of Christmas tree known to Hanna.

  🍂 However, her father, Albert Brandt, did not care much for the kind of tree everyone else liked. He looked for a bluish

Spruce

Stone Pine

tinge and a silver sparkle, which is what the Serbian spruce offers, and all the blue spruces such as the Colorado spruce. In those days, blue spruces were rare in Germany. They are not native in that part of the world, and the first saplings of the Serbian spruce were imported from the Balkans in the early years of the twentieth century and they did not spread until much later.

❧ Nor did Brandt insist on a rigidly symmetrical shape. In fact, he preferred irregularities in the tree's framework. Moreover, he thought the needles should be soft like a painter's brush and not necessarily numerous, and that their arrangements should be airy. He used to say that shimmering silvery-blue tones reflect both the skies above and the waters below. He argued that blue and silver are colors that transcend the earth's primary green, and he called the white of the snow the ideal, immaculate backdrop.

❧ Painter, woodsman, hunter, and trout fisherman, Brandt spent his life crisscrossing the forests of the Taunus Mountains north of Frankfurt. Although he said he did not like the idea of cutting down a live tree and taking it indoors for a brief spell of glory, he started looking for candidates as early as the spring. Two or three days before Christmas, he did finally cut down a tree—usually a small one that had been crowded in by bigger trees or was growing on a rocky, inhospitable ledge—and he brought it home dutifully in order to please his wife who came from the Black Forest, south of the Taunus mountains. And this was the second kind of Christmas tree Hanna has known.

❧ His wife agreed with him on his preference for blue and silver over the common green. But she was unyielding in her insistence on a live tree, cut down for Christmas, which was the tradition in her family.

❧ Albert Brandt was not religious, his daughter says, but "kind of worshiped God in nature." Over the years, he developed his own ritual of celebrating Christmas, by choosing a magnificent old spruce or pine he would declare the King of the Forest. Early in the morning the day before Christmas—he was accustomed to getting up at around three A.M.—he collected his three children and took them to the tree he had chosen for that year.

❧ The Brandt family lived in a house at the edge of the forest, and each year the father's choice was a different tree growing in another part of the woods. The tree not only had to have plenty of character and a bluish tint, but the setting had to be unusually beautiful, with a nearby creek and some rock outcroppings if possible.

❧ The walk to the King of the Forest was always long, at least half an hour, and he began taking his children along at about the time they reached the age of five. Hanna remembers that it was invariably very cold, and usually snowing. Her father showed them the tracks of deer and rabbit, and pointed to the sheltered nooks where the deer had slept. Almost every year, the children sighted a wild animal.

❧ On these occasions, Albert Brandt did not have a gun with him. Instead, he carried a box filled with candles and little metal candleholders. After they reached the King of the Forest that he had selected weeks earlier, he and the children put the candles on the branches, lit them, sang a few songs, and walked around the tree to keep warm.

❧ He talked about the probable age of the tree, the times it had lived through, and the reasons that might have caused the loss of branches. The children were more interested in finding out how much taller the tree might grow and how many more years it might live, and their father tried his best to answer those questions.

❧ Each tree he chose was truly a monarch, Hanna says. They were also the kinds of grand trees he used as models for his carefully detailed, old-fashioned landscapes. He painted rivers and mountains, colorful flower gardens and cloud-filled skies, winding dirt roads and wild animals in motion. But trees were his favorite subjects, and among them, he liked blue-tinted conifers best.

❧ Hanna's mother was never present at the tree

ceremonies—she said she was too busy preparing for Christmas—but she did wait for the children with a big breakfast. As the children grew older, they found out that she felt there was something vaguely un-Christian about the celebration in the forest. Indeed, Jesus Christ was not mentioned, and the homage paid to the great tree seemed to echo those pagan times when the tribes of Northern Europe feared the darkness that fell earlier every day and thought it propitious to welcome the day when the sun turned and the days started getting longer.

❧ As Hanna now thinks about it, the King of the Forest was her father's very own special Christmas tree, and the ritual he organized was a nature-worshiper's way of marking the passage through the dark season of winter.

❧ Father is gone, and so is mother. The woods of Hanna's childhood are now suffering from the encroachments of human habitation and industry. Acid rain has done much damage. But Germans still prefer the dense green Norway spruce for their Christmas tree.

❧ These days, in Washington, D.C., Hanna too paints, and she finds that her landscapes are not complete unless they are presided over by stately conifers in otherworldly hues of blue and silver.

23
A Real, Live Christmas Tree

Are you having trouble deciding between a traditional, symmetrical blue spruce that will become part of your trash two weeks after it serves as the focus of your Christmas, and an artificial Christmas tree of uncanny perfection, complete with cones and scent, that can be stored in the attic, then dusted off and reused every, year? Why not reject these options and invest instead in a real, live Christmas tree?

&❧ First decorating a live evergreen tree for indoor use and then planting it out in the yard is the ecologically responsible way of celebrating Christmas in our age of massive deforestation and rising air pollution. The risks are few, the satisfactions are considerable, and the price is usually less than thirty percent over what a cut tree costs.

&❧ A live tree is more expensive than a cut tree because of the extra work involved in digging out its rootball, which is nowadays done with a machine rather than with a spade. Sawing trees off at ground level is faster and easier, and so is storing and moving them around in a garden center.

&❧ Buying a live Christmas tree takes a bit of planning. It is wise to begin by calling a number of garden centers to

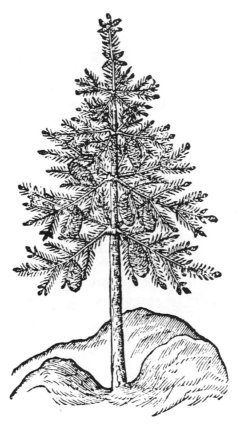

"Smaller Wild Pine"

check out what kind of Christmas trees they have balled-and-burlapped or in containers, and in what sizes.

&❦ One tree of choice that does well when planted out is the Norway spruce. Imported from Northern Europe in colonial times, it has since spread across the temperate region of North America and has become so much part of the landscape—or "naturalized" as the botanists say—that it is now considered a native.

&❦ The Norway spruce matches everyone's idea of a Christmas tree: slender and conical, with branches sweeping downward and dense needles. Its slim, pendulous cones are up to seven inches long, green when young and ripening to a handsome rusty brown. In the first ten years of its life, it can grow close to one foot a year, but its growth slows down considerably later on. Its eventual height may reach 150 feet, which means that a prudent homeowner will put it where there is plenty of room.

&❦ A slower grower and seldom going over a height of eighty feet is the Serbian spruce, a native of the Balkans that has spread across the Old World. It is a favorite Christmas tree throughout much of Europe. More reliably symmetrical than the Norway spruce, the Serbian spruce is dense and elegant. It is however a slow starter and needs full sun and good air circulation.

&❦ While Norway spruces are medium green—a kind of workaday green—and Serbian spruces have only a bluish sparkle, Colorado spruce is green to blue, with some varieties achieving a brilliant icy blue and an elegant whitish silver. Originally from the Rocky Mountains, the Colorado spruce is now planted across much of the country. Different varieties reach different heights, and show different hues.

&❦ Trees of the genus spruce (*Picea* in Latin)—particularly Norway spruce—have their disadvantages. They do not like pollution and are thus not ideal city trees. If planted in shade or crowded into groupings, they soon lose their lower branches, which makes them look leggy and not so attractive to people who seek balance and symmetry.

❧ Closely related to the spruces are the pines, which many evergreen aficionados prefer. While spruces are considered stiff in shape and hard to mix in with other trees, pines are regarded as soft, even fluffy, and easy to group with other trees.

❧ Probably the best-seller among live Christmas trees is the eastern white pine, easy to recognize because its needles come in bundles of five. The state tree of Michigan and Maine, it is airy, defiant of pollution and fast-growing, often reaching a height of one hundred feet, with tapered cones as long as ten inches.

❧ It is best to buy eastern white pine already sheared (pruned back). The extra charge for what is known as "a sheared pine" is well worth it because that initial shearing should be done by a knowledgeable person, when the young shoots are half grown, in late spring or very early summer, and in such a way that plenty of dormant buds are left below the cut. A sheared pine will have a better structure than one left unsheared.

❧ Not so tall and a slower grower is Scotch pine. Its twisted, bluish-green needles come sheathed in twos, and its bark is reddish.

❧ More important than the particular variety of a live Christmas tree is the treatment it should receive:

❧First and foremost, don't allow the rootball to dry out. It is a good idea to put the tree in a terra-cotta pot or some other container slightly larger than the rootball and then to fill the gap with peat moss that can be easily kept moist and frequently checked for dampness. Another way to conserve moisture is to keep the rootball in a plastic bag.

❧Don't keep the tree indoors longer than a week; ten days is extremely stressful. If the air indoors is dry—and it usually is for an evergreen—mist the tree daily and always make sure that its roots are well watered.

❧Avoid placing the tree near a radiator or other heat source, but also keep it away from drafts. The ideal place is an unheated closed-in porch, but since that is often impossible or impractical, at least keep the tree in a room where the temperature is under sixty-six degrees.

🍃Switch all the lights off at night. The combination of warm indoor temperature and the extension of daylight via electricity could prematurely break the dormancy that the tree probably entered before it was taken out of the ground. Buds breaking out—the beginnings of new growth—are the sure sign of a tree embarking on a new growing season, in the environment of a false spring. This environment can damage the tree. If buds do break out, it is best not to plant out the tree—the frost would kill all the tender new growth—but to store it in an unheated garage or some other place protected from killing frost.

🍃Dig the hole for the tree as soon as you buy it. Don't wait with the digging because it is hard to dig a hole after the ground freezes over.

🍃Cover the hole with a hefty piece of plywood lest someone stumble into it. It is also a good idea to keep a bag of topsoil, compost, or peat moss in the garage or some other place safe from freezing. It will come in handy at the time of planting out when some soft, porous material should be poured into the spaces around the rootball. A good soak after planting is indispensable.

🍃 Garden centers estimate that they sell five cut Christmas trees for every live one. Yet planting out one's Christmas tree is a great way of extending Christmas. For most of the twenty-first century, that tree will say Christmas 1992, or 1993, or whichever year it was when buying a live Christmas tree became a new family tradition.

24
Harold Baker's Signature

"I know that my husband was very fond of this tree," the new widow told Harold Baker. "And I did and I do appreciate your giving it to him years ago as a gift. I realize it is precious, but to me, it looks like a deformed Christmas tree. Would you mind taking it back?"

A tough, no-nonsense lawyer, Baker did not blink or blanch. He understood. For as long as he has grown his pines and spruces—about thirty years—almost everybody who laid eyes on them has asked questions like these: Why don't your trees look like Christmas trees? Don't you like straight trunks and nice, evenly spaced, symmetrical branches? Why do you grow evergreens that look as if Picasso designed them?

Baker groans, grunts, shrugs. In his seventies, he is beyond arguing with people who do not understand the finer things in life. He knows precisely what he likes and why; he thinks most of the rest of humanity do not. But he could not care less about setting them right.

By the entrance of Baker's 250-acre farm in Boyds, Maryland, stands a tree he is particularly fond of. He planted it years ago, and he acknowledges that it could serve as his signature: a weeping spruce less than five feet tall and shaped like a letter U turned upside down. It looks as if it had been drawn by someone with an unsteady hand. The branches are thickly covered with sturdy, short bluish-green needles. Behind the tree is a vista of acres of rolling pasture.

❧ "Isn't that a beauty?" Baker asks, without expecting a reply. "Just look at its lines, its drama, its sweep! It grows one inch a year, no more, and its shape gets more interesting as it grows. It is unpredictable. I look forward to seeing what it will do."

❧ What Baker means by "interesting" other people are likely to characterize as "crooked" or "contorted."

❧ He goes for what he calls "sculptured sweeps." He has a variety of spruce called Highlandia which sprawls on the ground, but some of its branches rise a foot high.

❧ "This piece reminds me of the waves of the sea," he says, pointing to one mature specimen. "But when you buy one of these already grown, first you must visualize where you will put it. This particular piece would look good next to a large rock."

❧ Near his nineteenth-century farmhouse nearly a thousand feet up the driveway, Baker has a collection of hundreds of rare and unusual conifers. They are all dwarf, which means that their branches add no more than an inch of growth a year, and they may never reach the height of eight feet. (Ordinary conifers, such as the eastern white pine or Leyland cypress, can grow as much as four feet a year and eventually reach the imposing height of one hundred feet.)

❧ Nor do Baker's conifers conform to any canon of symmetry or balance, Oriental or occidental. Some of the conifers have broad tops with hills and craters, or are almost flat; others have contours that suggest a crescent, a sail, or a fan. Still others grow in the shape of a candelabra.

❧ "I have every every kind of pine and spruce," he says, referring to two divisions of the conifer family. "But I can't tell you how many trees I've got total. I keep buying them whenever I travel."

❧ Each of the unusual shapes is a result of a *sport*—a

botanical term denoting a spontaneously occurring genetic variation, a departure from the standard form. Once a sport is identified, branches of it may be cut off and grafted onto sturdy common stock, which in the case of pines is usually the tough, robustly healthy eastern white pine.

❧ Unusual conifers are at least four times more expensive than the usual ones, and sometimes twenty times, partly because sports are relatively rare—one out of ten thousand or so—and partly because grafting conifers is a delicate operation that is not always successful. Conifers have a strange tendency to develop a fungus or start rotting around the spot where the graft is made.

❧ Baker has a strong preference for blue spruces, particularly the variety called Thompson, which he finds "the brightest blue." New growth on the Thompson blue spruce is indeed a brilliant, otherworldly blue sometimes called cerulean, but later the needles darken and turn somber. Baker also likes the variety called Montgomery, which is darker than the Thompson, and unlike landscape designers who are fastidious about evergreens—saying that some will not go together—Baker favors planting all the different tints of blue spruces close to one another.

❧ He has dozens of globe-shaped Colorado blue spruces grafted eighteen inches high on a naked trunk called the standard. Here the objective is a firm, perfectly round top.

❧ He also has eastern white pine grafted on a standard. "In a few years, it will develop a good, tight globe," he says. "But it is a slow process."

❧ Impatient with people and protective of his time, Baker is endlessly patient with plants. He likes them to grow slowly, disliking rapid growers. Strict and stiff when it comes to adhering to the letter of the law, he enjoys the unpredictable nonconformity of his evergreens.

❧ He is also interested in variegated or two-toned conifers. He has one spruce that offers a spectacular contrast of blue-green and silver needles—something of a space-age look—and another that is blue and white, which may seem like a conventional combination but is in fact quite rare.

  🖎 Baker buys the conifers when they are only a few inches high. He keeps them in whiskey barrels and in beddings where the soil has been loosened up and improved with plenty of woodchips, sand, and peat moss. He must improve his soil because his property features mixtures of heavy clay and Seneca sandstone, and the natural drainage is much too slow.

  🖎 Proper watering is crucial for conifers, particularly for those planted in containers. A few years ago, Baker installed a drip-irrigation system so his trees get just the right amount of water—not so little that they dry out, but not so much that they grow too fast.

  🖎 Baker believes that unusual conifers look their best "in splendid isolation" and are ideal for small townhouse gardens, fitting in well with a modern house and looking right in a Japanese-style garden.

  🖎 "Each piece is unique and makes a separate statement," he says. "But you don't need more than one unusual conifer in one garden. Two of them may already be too much."

  🖎 Another advantage of unusual conifers is that they do not overwhelm other vegetation. But Baker disagrees with the idea that his unusual conifers are unassuming. "There is nothing modest or mundane about my conifers," he declares. "Nothing at all."

  🖎 Baker is also a flower gardener, and his favorite flower is the daffodil. "I like daffodils because they complement my evergreens best," he says. He loves the sophisticated new hybrids that boast some pink in a blossom that is traditionally white or yellow. He is the proud owner of three expensive, avant-garde daffodil varieties that exhibit "true pure pink"—and not just an odd shade of orange which its hybridizer calls pink to be fashionable.

  🖎 To the question why he goes after pink, Harold Baker has a prompt, brusque answer: "Because daffodils are not *meant* to be pink."

25
Dreaming of a White Christmas Tree

In the 1930s, when Jim Horne was a small child on a farm near Statesville, North Carolina, he used to go to the woods with his father to cut a tree for Christmas. They did a lot of walking and looking and comparing before they finally agreed on a tree that had an array of dense branches and was also nicely symmetrical.

   🙌 "It had to be a fine, full tree," Jim Horne recalled a few years ago, "and so beautiful that we wouldn't have to decorate it at all. Because we didn't have money for decorations."

   🙌 Always, the tree was a Virginia cedar, which the Hornes and all their neighbors called an eastern cedar. Known as the poor man's Christmas tree, it was the only conifer that survived in the scraggly woods near the Horne farm.

   🙌 "Most people just hate eastern cedar," said Horne later, by then a retired Air Force colonel and a devout horticulturist. "Most people think eastern cedar is just scrub. 'It's everywhere,' they say, 'it's too common.' But what they don't know is that if you pamper eastern cedar, it becomes a stately, beautiful tree with a beautiful aroma."

   🙌 In the 1980s, living in an immaculate suburban home in northern Virginia, Horne tended a showcase garden in a spacious corner lot. Twice a year, usually during early spring and late, late fall, he fed his eastern cedars and the thirty-five other conifers he grew. He applied a couple of pounds of 5-10-5 fertilizer, which he poured down holes he had bored with a big auger around each tree. The top two inches of the hole he filled with what he called "really good compost," which he packed hard. He then threw more of that compost an inch or two thick around the base of the tree. Of course, the compost came from the pile he built and maintained.

🍃 But he did more than keep his conifers robust.

🍃 He was also dreaming of developing a white Christmas tree—not just pale green or silvery white, but true white, as if made of hoarfrost.

🍃 For some seven years, he experimented with various chemicals that he had reason to hope might perhaps induce an eastern cedar to sprout white rather than green needles. He applied extra doses of lime and iron tablets, and he added some other chemicals known to have a bleaching effect on foliage. Finally, by 1986, he produced one specimen, which eventually reached a height of ten inches, with a lot of white or at least whitish needles.

🍃 He was determined to turn most of the conifer needles white. Once that happened, he reckoned, he would propagate the tree by taking cuttings from those branches that developed the whitest needles.

🍃 Then, if those cuttings took root and sprouted needles that were white and stayed white—or, as botanists put it, if the plant retained the critical new characteristics—Horne would have created a new breed: a conifer with mostly or perhaps entirely white needles.

🍃 "There would be no more need for florists to spray paint on Christmas trees to make them look as if snow had fallen on them," Horne said. Nature, as assisted by Horne, would produce its own version.

🍃 Another fir tree Horne was fond of was Irish juniper. He had five of them, each cigar-shaped and some twelve feet high, standing like sentinels by the driveway to his terrace. He devised an ingenious solution for the problem of juniper branches dropping and breaking after a heavy rain or snow: he wrapped a nylon fishing line or waxed quilting yarn around the foliage. Extremely strong yet invisible, the cord kept the tree in its elegant shape.

He also nurtured twenty-four saplings of a rare Japanese dwarf cypress which he had propagated from a root cutting. According to the books, one is not supposed to be able to propagate this particular species that way, but Horne was interested in defying conventional wisdom, and he had a lucky hand.

A serious student of horticulture, Horne read books and periodicals and took courses. But what he enjoyed most was the manual craft of propagation by cuttings. He said his method was straightforward and had nothing to do with any mumbo-jumbo such as a so-called green thumb.

"You use both your thumb and the two fingers nearest your thumb," he said. "Then you make it pop. Just pop. It's that simple. But you also have to believe in what you are doing."

He inserted his cuttings into a "superrich" soil, which he kept "extremely moist" for ten days. He produced a lot of cuttings, most of which he gave away to friends and charitable organizations, such as his church.

Nevertheless, developing the white Christmas tree was the horticultural project closest to Horne's heart. "It's not really an obsession," he said, defending himself. "It's just something I'd like to do. I keep on trying. I fool around with this and that. I believe that a naturally white Christmas tree would be just beautiful. I know that people everywhere would love it. It's the sort of new thing, something a little different and unusual, that people look for."

Each year, Horne told his family and friends that, God willing, by the following Christmas he would have in pots five-inch-tall cuttings of his white Christmas tree. He did not see his dream come true. In November 1988, just before Thanksgiving, he died of cancer. His father died three months later.

❧ Jim Horne never tried experimenting with any evergreen other than eastern cedar. Nor did he plan to. He always remembered those long walks in the woods with his father, searching for the finest, the most beautiful eastern cedar.

❧ Half a century later, Jim was still looking.

26
Pyracantha: The Hussar Among Evergreens

A distant cousin of the apple tree and the rosebush, the pyracantha is cherished for its clusters of brilliantly colored berries set against an abundance of glossy green foliage that stays green all winter long in most of the United States. Also popularly known as firethorn, the pyracantha originated in China, and over the past century it has become a much beloved landscape plant in North America and in Europe.

➤ Whether a single plant standing in front of a picture window or a pair of identical twins set by the pathway to the house, the pyracantha is as lively and cheerful as a country cousin who uses swear words, yet at the same time it is as elegant as an aunt with long gloves who only shops at Lord & Taylor. Its branch structure is formal yet never stiff, and its leaves are well shaped. Pyracanthas look well tailored when planted close and used as a hedgerow, or as an espaliered tree trained against the house or a framework. They may also form a fine allée when a distance of six to ten feet is put between the plants.

➤ When composing an evergreen garden, a gardener ought to consider including the pyracantha because its visual impact is even stronger when combined in a design with spruces or hemlocks, pines or arborvitaes.

Pyracantha

❧ Planting pyracantha in early spring is ideal, but midfall is a good alternative. Since it is a sturdy plant and almost always sold and grown in containers, it may in fact be put in the ground at any time of the year.

❧ The best time to prune it is after flowering, but it may also be pruned in the spring if the objective is to achieve a certain shape. It does not take offense when pruned severely, though many pyracantha aficionados prefer its natural form. When the objective is to encourage more branches—or no branches at all in one particular direction—it is enough to use one's thumb and forefinger to rub out new growth in early spring.

❧ For one out of every two pyracantha admirers, the berry is what matters most. Pyracantha berries start as delicate, creamy-white blooms in May. With most varieties, the fruits ripen in August and persist until December—and even beyond. The colors of different varieties range from pale yellow through orange to carmine.

❧ The berries are all skin and seed—like a dried-up crab apple. Nevertheless, some gardeners do manage to make jam out of them, with a flavor that suggests the cranberry. Birds and squirrels eat pyracantha berries only after they turn soft, which happens early in the winter with some varieties and late, or not at all, with the new and improved varieties.

❧ The berry clusters are often so plentiful that the branches bend down with their weight. With some varieties the berries split open after a severe frost, but the new, improved varieties do not have that problem.

❧ For the past three decades, the National Arboretum has singled out the pyracantha as a major landscape plant that needs to be improved. The breeding program, led by botanist and pyracantha enthusiast Donald Egolf until his recent death, has thus far yielded half a dozen outstanding new varieties that outperform the traditional pyracanthas in all the categories that matter: disease resistance, reliable, evergreen foliage that stays on the plant, and long-lasting and brilliantly colored berries.

Moreover, the program has yielded new varieties with a range of growth habits previously unavailable in the genus.

❧ The first superior pyracantha was Navaho, released to the nurseries for propagation in the 1970s. A maximum of six feet tall and eight feet wide, with stems spread widely from the base, Navaho has a dense, compact, moundlike growth habit. It is ideal for a hedgerow or any other kind of massive barrier, but it also works as a handsome foundation plant. The orange-red berries ripen in November in large clusters of ten to fifteen and persist until late spring. North of the Mason-Dixon line, the Navaho needs to be planted in an area sheltered from wind; otherwise its foliage will turn brown after Christmas.

❧ Teton, which also reached the market in the 1970s, is the first pyracantha with an unmistakably vertical growth habit. It produces a narrow hedge without the need for much pruning, and it qualifies for small gardens and in tight corners. The berries, as many as thirty to a cluster, are an intense, gleaming orange.

❧ Both Navaho and Teton are resistant to scab—which turns the fruit black—and tolerant of fire blight, the disease that blackens leaves and kills twigs. Like its relative the pear, the pyracantha—particularly the traditional varieties—is susceptible to fire blight.

❧ If fire blight strikes, the affected branches must be cut off a foot or so below the place where the infection is noticed. After each cut, the saw or pruning shears used must be disinfected with rubbing alcohol or household bleach. If they are not, the blades will spread the disease.

❧ Spraying with Ferbam is recommended, first when the buds break open and then at regular ten-day intervals—much as the rosebush needs to be protected from blackspot.

❧ The variety named Apache is one of the products of the mid-1980s. It is a dwarf, intended for townhouse gardens. The Arboretum's original specimen has grown to five feet in height in fourteen years. It is wider than it is tall, and the growth is symmetrical, moundlike, admirably dense. The texture suggests the densely packed, small-leaved boxwood, and the harvest is a profusion of small red fruit: between twenty and sixty per cluster. The fruit ripens in August and persists until December.

🍂 Pueblo is the latest product of the Arboretum's breeding program. It has long, slender, glossy leaves and orange-red berries—as many as forty in a cluster. The branches are emphatically horizontal, and the mature plant is more than twice as wide as high. Pueblo is an ideal choice for a screen and a fence.

🍂 Both Apache and Pueblo have been selected from stock highly resistant to scab and fire blight. According to the Arboretum, there is no need to spray them with chemicals.

🍂 The Arboretum has not stopped working on pyracanthas. Until his sudden death in December 1990, Egolf kept hand-pollinating pyracanthas, and he was getting ready to release to the public some of his selected seedlings, which are either dwarf—intended for the small scale of many of today's gardens—or prostrate, usable as ground covers. He considered that further increasing resistance to scab and fire blight was the top objective of the improvement program.

🍂 Pyracanthas are easily propagated. They come up readily from their berries, but the berries first need to be what biologists call stratified: after they mature, they must be kept in a refrigerator—not the freezer—for at least three months, airtight in a polyethylene bag and buried in a sterile growth medium. But to get a replica of the mother plant, propagation needs to be done from six-to-eight-inch young branches. When the cuttings are dipped into a growth hormone, the plant will start growing lustily and fruit heavily as early as the second season.

🍂 In the winter landscape, the pyracantha stands out like a hussar in a dress uniform among infantrymen in fatigues. It is a happy choice for people who long for bright red berries to peek out of the snow and who look for a counterpoint to the grays and browns of winter.

Ways and Means

27
The Art of the Espalier

One particular genre of horticulture attracts both the thoroughly practical gardener looking for the resolution of problems such as lack of space and the ambitious artistic soul in search of a distinctive style to distinguish his or her garden: the espalier or "trellis," as the French word is translated. The espalier is a traditional technique of forcing and pruning trees and shrubs to grow flat against a wooden fence or a brick wall, or to conform to a design structured by a trellis, or to follow the pattern determined by parallel wires strung between wooden posts.

❧ An espaliered garden has a highly structured, geometrical appearance, and espalier aficionados have been known to go overboard by creating labyrinths of flowering trees that can end up looking something like a backdrop to a murder mystery. Yet no matter how elaborate an espaliered design may be, the technique is simple and surprisingly easy to learn. Widely practiced in the town gardens and farm orchards of Europe, espalier's origins may go back as far in time as pharaonic Egypt, or perhaps ancient Mesopotamia.

❧ Deciding on a particular shape and its means of enforcement constitutes the first stage of the project. The letter T with two or three additional horizontal bars is one of the basic espalier designs. Another is the letter U or V growing out of a vertical axis at an angle and repeated two, three, four, or even more times. Two formations of a long and narrow letter U are often grown on top of a broad T or Y. One of the showiest and most practical designs is the candelabra, usually with six branches but with thirteen branches in the case of one celebrated specimen, a pear tree well over a hundred years old growing in the Jardins du Luxembourg in Paris.

&. If the espaliered trees are placed side by side and particularly if they face one another—for instance, against parallel walls following a straight line—most gardeners find that the repetition of the same design looks better than a jumble of different designs.

&. It is best to start with a young tree, by tying its supple branches to a sturdy wooden scaffold, or to a system of heavy-gauge wires firmly and reliably anchored. Using a frame is much easier than nailing or boring holes into a wall of brick or stone. If you are afraid of fracturing a branch, tie it to a stiff wire and then bend it gradually in the desired direction.

&. The best fastening materials are soft string and raffia. But for less fastidious gardeners, rubber bands or even strips of old cotton bedsheets will do. Avoid wire, which may choke the plant's channels for moisture and nutrients. What matters is that the tie-up not be too tight and that it allows for an expansion of the branch. Be prepared for frequent loosening and retying.

&. Cutting off the tip of the newly planted tree is the way pruning traditionally begins. The objective is to encourage additional lateral growth. Next, remove those lateral branches that do not fit into the design. Then, and in the years to come, keep snipping selectively: permit those tips that grow in directions determined by the design to become branches; the rest should be pinched off as soon as they break out.

&. The easiest subjects for espalier are vigorous growers such as forsythia, pyracantha, winter jasmine, and holly. Among fruit trees, the favorites are apple, cherry, peach, and pear.

❧ Among the devotees of the espalier are gardeners who enjoy training and pruning a plant in a way that is similar to sculpting or practicing architecture. Though some gardeners condemn the enforcement of geometrical designs as a reactionary aberration and a form of plant repression, an espaliered fruit tree does undoubtedly offer significant practical advantages:

❧An espaliered tree is so flat as to be almost two-dimensional, thus saving space. Such a tree takes up about one-fifth of the space required by an ordinary tree.

❧The espaliered tree tends to produce superior blossoms and fruits. Botanists say that the reason is probably the uniformity in the branching structure, which allows an even flow of the sap. Moreover, the pruning produces more spurs for blooming and fruiting. Blooms are brighter and fruits ripen earlier when the tree is set against a south-facing wall of brick or stone. The wall screens the tree from the wind and reflects warmth.

❧Sunlight distribution and air circulation are far better than with a regular tree growing freely by itself or in an orchard.

❧Thinning the fruit and treating diseases is easier when facing the structure of an espalier instead of the layers of foliage on an ordinary tree of dense, bushy foliage. For the elderly and the very young, as well as for the handicapped, an espaliered fruit tree is an ideal plant to tend and to harvest.

❧Whether ornamental or fruit-bearing, an espaliered pear or cherry tree can cover and disguise a wall as effectively as any climber. It will "soften" and "embroider" a large blank space such as a garage wall, gardeners say. While clematis, silver lace vine, or wisteria can present a romantic tangle of foliage and blossoms, the effect of an espaliered plant's precisely parallel branches and blossoms is dramatic in a classically formal way.

❧ In the United States, gardeners have contributed to the culture of espalier by creating informal or free-form designs. The stated objective is to follow the natural development of a tree—letting it decide its shape with only a minimum of intervention by the gardener. A smart compromise between the traditional and the free-form design is the so-called natural fan, which emphasizes the most vigorous lateral branches.

❧ A whole garden of espaliered trees and bushes strikes many gardeners as too precious. The geometrical patterns of espaliered trees and bushes were most in fashion in Europe in the seventeenth and eighteenth centuries, under the influence of France's Louis XIV. The Sun King admired nature but preferred it regimented, under the control of a master thinker, and a garden of espaliered plants summed up his sentiments. Perfectly.

28
Trees of Passage

Next time you are in Europe in the summertime, walk up and down a leafy, tree-lined allée of lindens, poplars, or horse chestnut trees, then rest on a weathered wooden bench, and watch the passing show.

🐚 Under parallel rows of trees of the same species, the natives—Spaniards or Germans, Swedes or Bulgarians—take part in a ritual as old as civilization: a leisurely stroll of no particular destination. They start out as babies paraded in prams, then they run back and forth and sideways as children. A few more years pass, and they cruise, looking for partners, and then they loll arm-in-arm as lovers. Next they promenade as parents, and finally—how time flies!—as grandparents who love to talk about the time long ago when those great, spreading trees overhead were only slender saplings.

🐚 In a dictatorship, the best way to exchange thoughts is while sauntering along a shady lane, out of earshot of informers and away from microphones. Nothing appears as innocent as a slow, rambling walk under the city's trees.

🐚 Every year, there is a careful, thoughtful, sometimes severe pruning, which is part of civilization's overall strategy: a row of trees is a regulated forest where impulsive, haphazard growth must be made to conform to the ordered geometry of urban living.

❧ Life under the shade of stately trees is a *tableau vivant,* a precisely drawn etching, familiar from another century. Nobody will stop you if you jog. But, unmistakably, jogging is inappropriate. An allée is for the slow track, meant for solitary contemplation or conversation with friends.

❧ Observe the trees. They may be lindens—ovals of refinement, with heart-shaped leaves and an intoxicating scent from thousands of tiny flowers in July. Or magisterial oaks—venerated by the peoples of antiquity, and popular with children and squirrels because of the acorns, which vary much in shape and size, depending on the variety of oak. Or Lombardy poplars—slender, fast-growing, and luxuriantly leafy, but also tragically fragile and irresponsible with suckers. Or horse chestnuts—with exquisite spikes of flowers in May, to be followed by hundreds of nuts that look like chestnuts but are so bitter as to be inedible.

❧ The trees are planted six, twelve, or fifteen feet from one another, and the great parks such as Versailles and broad boulevards such as Berlin's Unter den Linden boast as many as four parallel rows of trees. But no tree is out of line. Ever.

❧ Grass is seldom grown in the shade of an Old World allée. Instead, the ground is often covered with a layer of pebbles. Stones no larger than a quarter are the most pleasant to walk on. A choice material is a round, smooth beach pebble, translucent or white, and smaller than a penny.

❧ The stone layer should be at least three inches deep, thus creating a no-maintenance path. If it is thinner, sooner or later the stones will sink into the ground and disappear. Bluestone dust, which costs about the same as sand, is a smart solution because it behaves much like cement, forming a layer that hardens and is inhospitable to weeds. Its grayish-blue color blends well with any vegetation, but Europeans find it too utilitarian, if not lower class.

🍂 A sophisticated effect may be achieved by covering the ground with sharply faceted crushed stone, the size and the color of sugar cubes. Gleaming white marble chips are expensive, but lend a Mediterranean elegance.

🍂 Before dumping stones in an allée, it is best to lay down a so-called landscape fabric, made of tough synthetic yarn and not affected by ground contact, which permits water to seep through but stops weeds from sprouting and stones from sinking.

🍂 The trunks of fine European allées are always straight and cleared of all lateral growth for at least six feet off the ground. Every year, branches are cut back, and some of them are eliminated. Europeans of all nationalities believe that overcrowded tree branches are esthetically unsatisfactory to humans and hygienically dangerous for trees. There must be lots of air circulating among the limbs, they say, and the tree's energy must be channeled into the sturdiest and the most promising half or one-third of the branches that sprouted. And, most important, they add, a tree has to be kept within limits and within reason, and never allowed to grow too high or too fast. Judicious pruning is of the essence.

🍂 "Why don't you Americans really prune your trees?" a Frenchman, a farmer in Normandy, once demanded of me. He believed that as a result of our weak-kneed permissiveness, our apples and pears are bland, our maples and sycamores grow too tall, only to be toppled by high winds. His apple and pear trees were cut back so much that in their leafless winter state they looked like stumps. The maples and sycamores on his property were carefully pruned, and their round and oval contours designed to soften the classic angularity of his eighteenth-century house.

🍂 To him, the typical American tree appeared overextended and unruly—and thus deeply uncivilized. "Americans still think they live in the wilderness," he said, and his pursed lips and arched eyebrows expressed a bemused disapproval. He was sipping the fifteen-year-old Calvados he had distilled from his apples, and his recipe also called for adding five percent pear to the mash. "Isn't it time that you Americans begin thinking that you have a civilization?"

🍃 His home province, Normandy, is proverbially conservative, celebrated for its marvelous apples and for its incomparable apple brandy, Calvados, which alone among all beverages may be consumed at any time during a proper French meal.

🍃 His farm has been in the family since the reign of Louis XVI—the unfortunate monarch who lost his head at the Place de la Concorde—and, he was proud to say, methods of cultivation haven't changed much since then. "We in Normandy believe that the more we cut back trees, the sturdier their structure becomes," he said solemnly. "In the case of apple trees, the more severely we cut them back, the tastier their fruit—and that is because the tree's élan goes into the fruit. Of course, there is a limit in pruning, as there is in everything. One must be reasonable when being drastic. But drastic one must be on occasion." Oh, the passions of reason that only reason understands!

🍃 In Normandy and elsewhere, the finest French allées have trees of the same height and girth, and, *bien entendu,* they are always of the same species. They recall an honor guard, or they form a tunnel, with the canopies of the two parallel rows embracing in the middle.

🍃 However, an allée need not be a thousand feet long to make a strong visual impact. A thirty-foot driveway lined with white-barked birches planted close together separates a garden from the street most effectively. While arriving in a well-designed garden suggests a visit to a private world, an allée prepares a visitor and communicates a sense of passage.

🍃 In America, several outstanding varieties of maple are used for allées: Crimson King (up to forty feet tall, with reddish foliage), Columnar Norway (up to seventy-five feet tall, with dark green leaves, and columnlike shape), and October Glory (vase-shaped and up to sixty feet). Ornamental pears, with lovely white flowers in the spring, are a good choice for people who like an allée of identical trees. On the other hand, ornamental cherry trees, while they too produce a blizzard of blooms, are far from having uniform structure.

❧ Also suitable for an allée is the pagoda tree (also called scholar tree), which is straight-trunked and increasingly popular. Vigorous and disease resistant, it has an oval crown of glossy green foliage and large trusses of white or yellow flowers in late summer. The variety called Regent Scholartree is now the preferred tough street tree planted in European as well as American cities.

❧ Taking the place of the native American elm, ravaged by Dutch elm disease, is the Japanese zelkova. Varieties such as Village Green are graceful substitutes, with fast growth, a wineglass shape, and exceptional hardiness.

❧ Planting an allée requires a lot of choosing, planning, and digging. But the result can be a warm introduction to a noteworthy garden. And, as the Europeans have always known, it can also be a memory lane.

29
Homeowner, Spare That Tree!

Homeowner, spare that tree! Cut off all that is dead and damaged, excessive and offensive, but give the tree a chance to come back!

❧ A crownless tree has a story to tell, as does one that has lost several limbs and is consequently lopsided, or one that has been reduced to a ruin of a broad trunk and a few whips rising from it. Such trees have come through the storms of winter and summer. They have prevailed, and it is encouraging for a human being to observe that their lust to live is undiminished.

❧ Getting rid of a tree is hard on one's finances and sometimes the emotions as well. Depending on its size, accessibility, and proximity to the house, cutting it down by professionals may cost anywhere between $500 and $5,000. Eliminating the stump is also a major undertaking that can easily add another $1,000 to the bill. Moreover, the site looks strangely, even eerily empty without the tree you have been accustomed to looking at. Unmistakably, something important is missing, and whatever that is, it is more than the shade the tree provided.

❧ Replacing a mature, well-established tree is not a simple

matter. If you want more than the standard four-to-six-foot-tall sapling, a tree can cost hundreds of dollars and setting it into the ground is a feat of engineering.

ᴥ Then, after all the trouble and expense, a new tree put in place of the old often gives clear signs of disliking the location it was given. A rational explanation is that during all those years that the old tree lived, it depleted the soil around it of nutrients. After digging up a large area and removing leftover roots—which might have attracted unwelcome insects, grubs, and bacteria—the prudent gardener will insist on adding plenty of good soil.

ᴥ The alternative to getting rid of a tree that for one reason or another does not give satisfaction is restructuring it. Perestroika in arboriculture is achieved by radical pruning, based on the principle that healthy new growth is stimulated at or near the point of a cut.

ᴥ One school of pruning recommends giving new life to an old tree or bush by the drastic program of removing one-third of the older growth each year. Overgrown shrubs are often chain sawed to ground level, which encourages plenty of new growth and gives an opportunity to shape the shrub.

ᴥ Whether the pruning is deliberate—for the purpose of training a tree and eliminating unwanted branches—or a consequence of a storm that did much damage, the tree will usually try to compensate for its losses of limb and twig by sending out plenty of new shoots. The reason has to do with the roots: they are unaffected by the losses above the ground, and they keep supplying the same amount of nutrients to a much reduced volume of foliage.

ᴥ Frequently, fresh growth following drastic pruning is exuberant, even excessive, and some of the aggressive whips must be eliminated to let the tree's energy concentrate on a few branches. Esthetic considerations as well suggest a structure based on a few strategically placed branches.

ᴥ A tuft of whips looking like a hedgehog or a witches'-

broom tends to rise out of stubs, which are short limbs that experts suggest must be avoided at all cost. They make a tree look like a hat rack and they siphon off the flow of nutrients.

🐌 The cut that experts nowadays recommend as ideal leaves a small ring collar. Recent research has determined that the critical defensive chemicals that seal a wound and rebuff fungi and insects are concentrated in the part of the branch that is closest to the point where it emerges from a thicker branch or the trunk. If the cut is flush—which was the standard advice only a few years ago—diseases enter and penetrate easily. So the cut now recommended can be described as "nearly flush." It calls for a "collar" of an inch or so.

🐌 It is important that all dead and damaged branches be removed as soon as possible. Otherwise, all kinds of fungi, insects, and diseases will attack the tree at the vulnerable points of the fracture.

🐌 Here are some more rules of pruning to remember when sawing parts of a decaying or storm-damaged tree:

🐌Eliminate branches that cross and rub against one another.
🐌Because branches at a wide, or obtuse, angle are stronger than those at acute angles, saw the latter if there is a choice.
🐌Whenever possible, make the cuts at branch junctions.
🐌When making a cut, saw parallel with the branch that will be left alone.
🐌Cut back long twigs to where a bud is forming.
🐌Remove larger branches at branch unions.
🐌Control the direction of new growth by eliminating rivals to branches that head in the direction you favor.

🐌 Before pruning, it is worthwhile to analyze your feelings about symmetry and asymmetry. Symmetry is an esthetic principle beloved by many great gardeners, past and present. It was carried to perfection—or excess, depending on one's judgment—by the French landscape architects of the seventeenth and eighteenth centuries, who left behind parks such as Versailles. Their grand designs were said to be based on logic and in pursuit of order, and they were meant to satisfy the intellect by aligning nature into a balance of circles and triangles, straight lines and precise curves, all of them repeatedly mirroring one another. (Some psychiatrists maintain that an insistence on symmetry goes back to our desire to love both of our parents equally.)

&. Asymmetry, for which a preference is often acquired late in life, has its acolytes too, and perhaps none as devout as the gardeners of Japan. Some of those who argue for asymmetry in the garden praise the delicacy of the imbalance implied in a skillful demonstration of asymmetrical design; others call asymmetry a higher form of balance.

&. In pruning a tree, cut to please yourself.

30
The Kindest Cuts of All

One grand strategic gardening activity is best pursued in wintertime: pruning bushes and trees. During winter, all woody plants are dormant, which means that when they are cut, there is no "bleeding" or "weeping" whatsoever, as there usually is in the spring, when the sap rises, and even in late summer, after the branches complete their annual growth cycle. Most experts agree that any oozing out of the sap weakens a plant, and a heavy loss can be dangerous.

❧ To prune, it is important to choose a day when the temperature is above freezing. When woody growth is frozen through, it is brittle, and saws or shears can easily shatter the tissue, the jagged edges of which then become vulnerable to insects and infections.

❧ Some gardeners think of sawing and cutting branches as unnecessary meddling. In their judgment, except for removing dead, broken, and damaged parts of a tree—and perhaps a few obviously weak, spindly branches—Mother Nature can be trusted to do a better job than the best-educated tree surgeon.

❧ However, the vast majority of those who work with trees and bushes firmly believe in the wisdom of vigorously cutting back branches in wintertime (and sometimes in the fall) as well as pinching out tips of stems in the spring. Pruning is not torture and mayhem, they say—to the contrary, it is a way to make better use of a plant's energy and to realize its potential.

❧ The fundamental, age-old principle of pruning is that every time a woody plant is cut, growth is stopped in one direction and encouraged in another. Experience suggests that particularly when it comes to trees that produce flowers or fruits, a judicious pruning program will yield more abundant harvests. And for gardeners it is plain common sense that thinning out overly exuberant growth will focus the plant's energies in a few directions and result in more vigor in the parts left unpruned.

❧ In wintertime, when the leaves are off, the basic framework of a tree, known as scaffolding, comes into plain view. Even a cursory examination reveals which branches extend too far or in the wrong direction. It is easy to identify and to eliminate branches that should not be, such as those that cross and rub each other; root suckers, a cluster of whips rising out of the roots or not much above them; and water sprouts, vigorous vertical growths that often emerge in clumps.

❧ During winter, it is easier to make decisions on the basis of what corrections are needed for a healthier and esthetically more satisfying structure. An examination on a fine, sunlit day will reveal which limbs may be upsetting the tree's symmetry or balance. Clearly, branches should not grow too close to the ground, and for most trees it is better not to spread too wide.

❧ A more difficult decision has to do with safe height. Some trees, maples for instance, grow too tall too fast, and a lanky, spindly tree becomes a target during those fierce summer wind storms.

❧ When pruning, gardeners tend to have in mind three principal models. The first, and most common, is the shape dominated by a sturdy upright trunk in the center, called the *central leader*. Among fruit trees, apple and pear trees grow naturally in this way. The advantage is that branches issue from the trunk at wide angles, which makes for a strong, healthy joint. To many gardeners, a tree with a robust straight trunk seems the ideal. In some instances, however, it is advisable to cut back the top of the central leader. Two welcome consequences follow: the tree will not grow too tall and no leafy canopy will develop to cast a shadow over the rest of the tree.

❧ The second shape, called the *modified leader,* emerges when the central leader is cut off early and several branches issue from it sideways. The result is a bushy growth, and its advantage is a better distribution of sunlight.

❧ The *open top*—also known as the *vase*—is the third of the best-known principal shapes. Without a central leader, the result is an open center that allows plenty of sunshine and good air circulation.

❧ Regardless of the model followed, thinning out dense growth produces a healthier tree. Whether the branches removed are misshapen or out of place, weak or too vigorous, it is important to keep in mind that new growth will take their places. Pruning stimulates fresh growth, and an overgrown old tree or bush may be rejuvenated when it is cut back severely and reduced to a few principal limbs.

❧ Pruning a large old tree is not a job for an amateur, because more is involved than creating a sculpture or rescuing a house from a monster limb that towers over the porch. Only a competent arborist has the knowledge and the equipment to tackle a fifty-foot-high red maple with an intriguing shape. It is best to call several tree surgeons recommended by friends and neighbors who were satisfied with their performance. The objective is not just to compare bids and go for the lowest. Pruning an old tree involves a series of decisions. Between homeowner and arborist, there ought to be mutual confidence and an understanding about the big job at hand.

31
The Treeman Cometh

The bell rings. Standing a few steps from the threshold is a big, burly fellow with a knitted cap pulled down over his ears and a chain saw in his hand. He and his men happen to be working in a neighbor's yard, he says, and they would be glad to check out your trees as well.

🍂 If no expert has looked at your trees for the past several years and if you have noticed some decay, or a surprising volume of growth, it may be a good idea to continue the conversation. Winter is the right time for tree work, provided that it is not under ten degrees Fahrenheit. Extreme cold makes the wood dangerously brittle.

🍂 First, ask the burly fellow for a business card and proof of insurance. The card may have "Fully Insured" printed on it, but it is wise to ask for a certificate that specifies how the homeowner is covered in case of damage to the property—such as a branch falling on the house or a smashed fence. You may place additional confidence in the company if the man shows workman's compensation insurance forms and displays a card showing membership in the National Arborist Association or in the International Society of Arboriculture. Both organizations concern themselves with high levels of workmanship, safety, and arboricultural research, and their members call themselves arborists. Other descriptions for the tree professional include treeman (simple and direct) and tree surgeon (somewhat uppity).

🍂 If your man clears all these hurdles, accompany him on an inspection tour of your trees and ask the sort of work that he—or in a rare case she—thinks may be required. Ask for a precise list of the work to be performed and the total amount charged. Make sure it is clear who does the cleanup, and where and in what state the logs and the brush will be left on your property.

🍂 It is not too much to ask that the logs be cut up in two-foot lengths and stacked in a pile next to the garage or by the air conditioner. On the other hand, the crew's readiness to haul away the wood should not increase your cost because they can sell most wood, unless it is so decayed that it is soft. But it is unreasonable to expect the removal of an eighteen-inch-diameter stump down to ground level. Grinding the stump requires an expensive machine and can cost several hundred dollars.

🍂 Reputable companies readily provide a written, itemized list of jobs to be performed, and the total to be charged. Misunderstandings have been known to arise on the issue of the amount to be charged *per* tree as opposed to the *total*. Most tree companies do not ask for any payment in advance. But the approximate starting and finishing dates are usually specified.

🍂 After the tree survey and the job proposal are completed, you need not sign on the dotted line. It is standard operating procedure to check on the treeman's reputation, and an obvious first step involves a walk over to the neighbor's house to find out what kind of work he has done.

🍂 The best kind of recommendation for a tree company is to have a number of satisfied customers in your own neighborhood over a long period of time. The ideal treeman is the one who has worked on the trees in your neighborhood for years, perhaps a generation. You can consider yourself uncommonly lucky if your neighborhood has a wise old pro coming around a few times a year who has seen those trees grow up and will prove it by talking about them, usually at great length. He knows their strengths and weaknesses; how fast they grew, and how they reacted to killer storms, insect infestations, and soil deficiencies.

🌺 Surveying the work performed in someone else's yard, you ought to look for pruned branches. Short stubs and cuts flush with the trunk are two telltale signs of inexpert work. Stubs are thwarted, frustrated limbs that tend to develop sprouts called witches'-brooms, and their wounds often do not heal. At the other extreme are flush cuts. Once standard in the industry, flush cuts are now considered damaging to the tree's health. The best research currently available declares that the so-called ring collar or ridge around the branch contains the chemicals that help seal the wound and fight fungi and rot and that the collar must not be removed.

🌺 Evidence that the workers "topped" a tree—sawed off the top of its trunk—ought to disqualify the company forthwith. Such treatment is acceptable as an extreme measure only if the tree trunk is rotten, about to split open, or threatens to keel over.

🌺 It is important to feel comfortable with the philosophy of your treeman. Does he look for balanced cuts and does he take into consideration the tree's beauty and integrity? Or is his main objective to "get it down to size"?

🌺 Pruning trees is dangerous, difficult, and expensive. Different treemen have different approaches, and it is possible to have two respectable professionals sharply disagreeing on the need to cut down a half-rotted tree. Particularly if the job is big or the tree is important, it makes sense to ask for three or even more opinions and estimates. Moreover, listening to experts on the subject of tree growth and care is the best way to educate yourself—even if the treeman's tale runs too long, and the homeowner, like Coleridge's wedding guest, "cannot choose but hear."

🌺 Pruning is far from qualifying as a science. For instance, reputable experts disagree on the need for pruning paint to be applied over cut surfaces: some say a chemical seal is necessary to stop infection and others trust the tree's own resources. There are also different theories on how to slow down or encourage growth.

🌢 Living and dealing with trees is a sensitive human enterprise, and strong attachments to theories and strategies develop as naturally as the tree grows in different directions. Professional counsel as well as hunches and premonitions should be respected and taken into account—particularly when the feelings are the owner's.

Decline and Fall

32
How Not to Be Stumped

For inveterate sentimentalists, a stump may be something of a monument: a gothic ruin of a tree that once was. But almost everyone else who cultivates a garden will readily conclude that something needs to be done to get rid of a tree stump, and as soon as possible. For gardeners determined to make use of every square foot of land, a stump—whether in the middle of a lawn or at the edge of the property—is at best a useless obstacle to progress and at worst a damned eyesore.

🍂 If one has access to a 24-horsepower tractor and a winch with chains and spikes, expert hands at the control can do wonders in extracting a stump from the earth. Family and friends should be invited to observe such a spectacle, which is more fun to watch than a tug-of-war. But a stump with roots thick and deep can prove immovable.

🍂 The one irresistible antistump force is a machine called a grinder. Most tree companies own one, but it is not a tool usually rented out. It is a brutally powerful device that grinds up the stump so that nothing of it is left above the ground. The resulting product is sawdust—a fine, lacy mulch that disintegrates within a season or two and helps to loosen up a flower bed's heavy soil.

🍂 To have a stump ground up costs at least ten dollars per inch of its diameter, provided that the truck carrying the grinder—which weighs well over a thousand pounds and is about as big as one-third to one-half of a Volkswagen Beetle—can park right next to the stump. The charge goes up dramatically if the grinder has to be carried to the stump by hand.

🍂 Most tree companies charge a minimum. If there is more than one stump, a lower price may be negotiated. If the stump is hefty and is ten feet or farther from a place that a truck can reach, it is a good idea to speak to as many as half a dozen companies. Perhaps one of them has in its arsenal a crane that will hoist the grinder onto the stump so that the cost will not remind you of a hospital bill for major surgery.

🍂 According to experts, the nutrient value of ground-up wood is close to zero. They warn that if it is used as a mulch, the disease that killed the tree could be transmitted. One such disease is verticilium wilt, which attacks a variety of plants from maple trees to tomatoes. Since it is no easy job to determine if a tree died of an infectious disease or just plain old age, it is the better part of wisdom not to use ground-up wood near trees and vegetables. However, experts add, regardless of what caused the tree's death, a mulch composed of its stump is safe for flower beds.

🍂 Considering the cost of grinding up a stump, letting it rot seems like a sensible laissez-faire policy. However, the gardener should face up to the possibility that a stump's complete disintegration may take as long as twenty years, particularly if the tree fell in a storm and its stump inherited a healthy root system that keeps feeding it—which is often the case with maples, for instance.

🍂 The process of rotting can be accelerated. The simplest and esthetically most pleasing strategy is to bury the stump under several inches of good soil and use the resulting mound for a lawn or a flower bed. Experts caution that there is no scientific evidence that such a soil cover will result in a more rapid disintegration of the stump, but from the few stumps I have seen treated that way, the evidence is convincing enough for me. One expert concern is that if the stump is buried, those bacteria and fungi that need air will not be able to participate in breaking it up. To let as many organisms as possible do their work, it is a good idea to use soil made airy by the addition of peat moss or some other soil lightener.

 ❧ Using the stump as a pedestal for one's favorite potted plants is a time-tested option. Though again there is no scientific proof, it does appear that the areas of the stump underneath the pots will rot faster than those without pots placed on them.

 ❧ A more aggressive strategy that works well is to plant a bush directly into the stump. The job is easy if the stump has a rotted middle, which is often the case with oaks and maples. An excellent candidate for such an unorthodox planting is creeping juniper, a vigorous evergreen that will spread its roots through every crack and crevice and widen them, thus speeding up disintegration. The juniper will make use of the nutrients of the rotting tree and blanket the largest stump in a few seasons.

 ❧ If the stump provides no natural cavity for planting, it is easy to make one the size of a highball glass or even a wine bottle, with the help of an electric drill and perhaps a chisel. The cavity should be filled with good topsoil, and frequent watering is recommended, both for the sake of the plant and for faster stump decay.

 ❧ Of course, there is always the option of using the stump as a base for an outdoor tabletop, be it wood or flagstone.

 ❧ Yet another possibility, particularly for the laid-back gardener, is to wait for sprouts to emerge from the stump. If the tree was felled by a storm and the roots are vigorous, clumps of broomlike growth are likely to come up from the bark near the wounded surface. Technically, these growths are suckers that one would normally cut off so that they do not siphon off the tree's energy needed elsewhere. But the tree no longer needs protection, and for some people these suckers are signs of persistence and desperation, and as such have an appeal beyond the merely esthetic. In the book of Job, God's chosen victim, the Bible explains: "For there is hope of a tree; if it be cut down it will sprout again . . . though the root thereof wax old in the earth, and the stock thereof die in the ground, yet through the scent of water it will bud, and bring forth boughs like a plant."

33
A Plum Tree's Last Hurrah

The plum tree in my backyard had the best spring of its four years of life. The immaculate white blossoms broke out early, but fortunately not so early as to be killed by a late frost. The long, slightly arching branches unencumbered with side growth and graced with petals were as dramatic as any featured on a classical Chinese painting. Once the petals fell on a balmy, summerlike afternoon—and the strong wind made that event look like a snowstorm—the fruits formed promptly.

ã The plums were about as large as an olive when I noticed one morning that the hitherto flat leaves had curled up—all of them. The fruits—so smooth, plump, and promising only a few days earlier—had acquired wrinkles. In a few more days, the leaves shriveled and then withered, and the fruits looked like miniature dried prunes. Unmistakably, the tree was dead.

ã What went wrong? Why the sudden death of a lovely, apparently healthy tree?

ã The location could not have been a problem. The tree had plenty of sun, which is a basic, nonnegotiable demand of fruit trees. The soil, while dominated by clay, had reasonably good drainage. The pH factor—that mysterious number that expresses acidity if it is less than 7 and alkalinity over 7—was

Plum

about 6.5, which is the kind of slight acidity that plum trees and most other fruit trees require. (When growing fruit trees, it is advisable to check from time to time lest the pH fall too low, meaning more than necessary acidity. The insufficient growth of nearby flowers is a danger signal of too much acid content.)

❧ Experts say that ninety percent of tree fatalities are due to water problems: either too much or too little. Fruit trees start rotting if the water collects around their trunks or roots. On the other hand, an extended dry season may also kill them. If there is not enough rainfall, irrigation is necessary, particularly at a time when the fruits begin to swell, and to a lesser extent throughout their growth.

❧ But my plum tree did not have water problems. Nor did it have winter injuries such as limbs cracked by ice or bark split, wounds inviting insects and bacteria that in turn lead to decay. Nor had I been guilty of feeding the tree in the fall with a fertilizer too rich in nitrogen, a diet producing a quick and often luxuriant growth which however does not have the time to acquire winter-hardiness. The growth dies back after the first frost, and many weak, sensitive trees cannot cope with the strain and succumb during their winter dormancy or in early spring.

❧ I checked for holes that are made by borers, such as the peach borer, but found no evidence of infestation. (To prevent the entry of borers that weaken and eventually kill a tree by disrupting its water delivery system, experts recommend twice spraying the trunk with an insecticide, first in July and then in August.)

❧ An intriguing hypothesis was advanced by Frank Santamour, a tree expert at the National Arboretum. "Many trees die because of graft incompatibility," he said. Santamour explained that the marriage between the rootstock and the scion may be happy for as long as ten years, but then suddenly the cells at the point of the graft union die in great numbers. The result is that the tree's internal plumbing is blocked, and water is no longer transported from the roots upward.

🍂 There is no explanation for the sudden switch-off of compatibility, Santamour says. But the problem is easy to identify: the usually visible ring a few inches above ground where the rootstock received the scion shows an indentation similar to a belt trying to contain a potbelly. Instead of the nearly seamless growing together of the two barks, a separation takes place, and the gap that develops between the two is sometimes so wide and deep that the blade of a steak knife will easily disappear in it.

🍂 Most fruit trees, particularly plum and peach trees, are grafted. The stock determines the height, which is important to most homeowners who prefer a dwarf or semidwarf tree to a giant that will take up too much space. Grafted trees are also capable of yielding huge quantities of fruit.

🍂 However, my plum tree's point of graft union showed no evidence of growing apart.

🍂 The most common reason for the sudden death of a tree, particularly a fruit tree, is a fungus, says Ron Korcak, an expert at the Beltsville research center of the U.S. Department of Agriculture. Korcak blames one of the many species of the soil-borne fungus *Phytophthora* as capable of attacking the roots and the trunk's connecting tissue underneath the bark. Once all the tissues carrying water and nutrients are cut off, the tree may die overnight—literally of thirst and hunger.

🍂 Korcak says that phytophthora is the cause of death if an incision into the trunk at about soil level shows a browning of the tissue or cambium, underneath the bark. He adds that there is nothing that can be done to prevent the spread of the fungus, which is invisible. (The only practical advice he could think of is that it is unwise to plant a new tree in the spot where another tree died, or even in the immediate vicinity.)

🍂 I performed the autopsy, but found no evidence of browned tissue.

🍂 Both Santamour and Korcak readily acknowledge that in many cases it is not possible to tell why a tree died suddenly. They also agree that a tree's finest moment often comes just before it dies, whether from draft incompatibility or a fungus attack, or for some unknown reason. Yes, the last blossoms are the loveliest, and the crop the year before tends to be the tree's very best.

❧ For those of us troubled by our inability to understand what caused the death of a tree, that swan song, that last hurrah—that final triumph—ought to be consolation.

34
The Death of a Tree

At about 7:30 A.M. on a raw day in March 1980, I was changing my daughter's diaper on the living room couch when I heard a great dull thud immediately followed by an ominous rumble, and a second or two later, screams from my wife and two sons who were having breakfast in the kitchen.

❧ I ran to the kitchen and through the window I saw our huge maple tree lying across our backyard, with the tops of its branches reaching over to our neighbor's lawn. A haze of fine gray dust rose ever so slowly from the trunk and hovered a foot or so above; it seemed like the spirit of the tree.

❧ Suddenly, it was very quiet. There was no wind whatsoever, and the stillness was eerie.

❧ We all stepped outside and stood speechless by the tree's upended roots, now strangely upright. The maple was the largest and the oldest tree in our backyard, standing about a hundred feet tall, and its trunk at the base measured some five feet across. It had cast a shade over most of the yard. Now it was dead, laid out on the lawn; its knobby roots, broken off at about three feet and as thick as a thigh, were now exposed, with clods of dirt clinging to its hairlike fibers. The tree made kindling out of everything in its wake: branches of other trees and shrubs, the swing set made of solid oak two-by-fours, and the children's cedar playhouse.

❧ Within minutes, our backyard was filled with neighbors. One of them, from across the street, happened to be picking up her newspaper on the front stoop when she saw the tree that loomed over our house "just disappear." Others heard the thud and the rumble, looked outside, saw a large gap in the canopy of branches and rushed to examine what happened.

❧ A small crowd of us decided to inspect the tree up close. We just stood there, staring at it, and nobody could say anything except to repeat that if, God forbid, the tree had fallen in the other direction, our house would have been crushed. It took several minutes before the children could bring themselves to step on the dead tree, but once they did, they climbed all over its upper branches, which had suddenly become accessible, and then kept running up and down the trunk that had stood so proud only a short while ago.

❧ We called the treeman we usually deal with and left a message for him to come over as soon as he could. But even before he called us back, in fact shortly after we had finished our breakfast, one fellow in padded overalls identifying himself as a tree surgeon presented himself at the door. Twenty minutes later came another. We never learned how they found out about the drama in our backyard because they were not very communicative. The first man told us that for $1,000 in cash he and his men could start sawing up the tree immediately. The second man's price was $600, but, he warned us, completing the job might take him longer than just a few days, because the trunk was unusually wide and there might be problems, in which case his price would go up. He did not specify the nature of the problems or the additional charge.

❧ Our veteran treeman showed up the next morning, inspected the tree, and looked almost as shocked as we had.

He declined to offer a bid because, he said, he did not have enough men and the right equipment to handle a trunk so wide.

᪥ We called two more tree companies, and their bids were in between what the first two men had offered. Three days later, we ended up hiring four hefty youngsters who said they lived not too far away and that they had been football players in the nearby high school. They worked for a day and a half, broke the chains of their saws several times, cursed profusely, and left with $400.

᪥ We walked around in a daze for days. In office and in school, on the street and on the phone, we could not talk about anything without mentioning what had happened to our tree.

᪥ We didn't forget to call the insurance company. The agent asked if the tree had been dead at the time of its fall. Not as far as we knew, we said, but it was March, and trees had not started to leaf out as yet. The agent asked us to cut into the roots, and we discovered that indeed they were dry, lifeless, dead. In that case, the tree was dead at the time of its fall, the agent concluded, and we had no choice but to agree.

᪥ We were then told that our insurance coverage did not extend to the cleaning up of a tree that was dead prior to its fall. But we were to be compensated for the value of whatever the tree had crushed.

᪥ Insurance policies on trees vary, we learned, but ours was pretty much standard. It may or may not matter if the property owner knows whether or not the tree was dead prior to its fall. And wind and storms matter in some policies and not at all in others. The damage trees cause when falling over your property and your neighbor's is a complicated legal affair. Check out the fine print, our friendly insurance agent advised; it's all there.

᪥ Our treeman, who had worked in the neighborhood for many years and knows every tree, stopped by for a postmortem. He told us that it is almost impossible to foretell when a tree will keel over. He had been aware of insects working their way into our tree, but he had thought that the chemicals he'd applied during the past ten years would take care of that problem. In retrospect, it was clear that he had been wrong, he readily acknowledged, because far more of the tree had rotted away inside than he would have suspected. But in our case, events followed a worst-case scenario that responsible treemen—most of whom are optimists, he suggested—do not like to act upon. As far as he could determine from poking a live tree from the outside and cutting off some dead and diseased branches, he would not, repeat not, have recommended cutting it down.

He thought that our tree was definitely older than the house, which was built in 1926, probably as old as this century, and that it was originally part of the hardwood forest—mostly maples and oaks, sycamores and American chestnuts—that had once stretched across the neighborhood, from what is now the American University down to Georgetown and the Potomac River.

But why did our tree die? we asked.

"Its day had come," was the best explanation the treeman could offer.

Other experts disagreed. One Ph.D. in forestry thought the tree had gotten much too tall. A colleague of his countered that in our neighborhood trees are well established and grow to great heights, and that it is all right in most cases, though of course not all.

Why can't scientists give us answers? Their well-educated doubts are far less satisfying than our instinctive guesses. We found the uncertainty unsettling. We live in the shade of giants we admire, yet we do not know when they might fall.

There are however a few danger signals we can read and should look for:

A tree is under stress if its leaves turn brown or yellow before fall, or drop prematurely, before the leaves of other trees turn their usual autumnal hue.

ஃIf the bark turns flaky or starts peeling, borers, or other pests might be burrowing deep into the tree.

ஃThe appearance of dead branches and twigs may mean rotting or insect damage.

ஃOozing on the trunk suggests root rot or an infection in the trunk.

ஃBranches without foliage indicate the presence of fungi or bacteria.

ஃ A visual inspection of your tree once a month is a smart idea. For instance, curled-up or wilted leaves during a dry spell in the summer or fall will tell you that the tree is suffering. Letting the hose run for half an hour all around the trunk of a hundred-foot giant is not excessive. The same treatment is called for before the first frost, and many experienced gardeners give a good soak to their trees during the winter whenever there is a few days' worth of thaw.

ஃ If you find leaf discoloration, dead branches, unhealthy bark, or oozing, the best thing is to call your treeman. But even if there are no visible problems, it makes good sense to have your trees checked out every two to three years, and the fall is the best time for a checkup. Spring is the second-best time, just as the first leaves appear.

ஃ Long ago we burned in our fireplace the last logs from that fallen maple tree, and the dogwood that sprouted only a few feet from the maple's five-foot-diameter trunk is now twenty feet tall and spreading wide. The daughter whose diaper I was changing the day our tree fell is now in junior high.

ஃ Yet to this day, one way of measuring time in my family is to remember whether something happened before or after the great maple fell across the backyard.

ஃ One of the attractions of planting annual flowers is that their demise at the end of the growing season is so implicit that we need not think about it. We routinely yank out petunias, zinnias, marigolds, and nasturtiums after they are killed by frost and toss them on top of the compost pile. Then, when spring comes, we plant in their places something new and different, like a salvia the color of paprika. Or we go back to the familiar old varieties once again.

❧ When we are dealing with annuals, the word death seems inappropriate. Things get only a little more complex with herbaceous perennials, the category of plants that die down to the ground in the fall or winter but sprout again from their roots the following spring. Occasionally, a herbaceous perennial fails to return, and the gardener is miffed, blaming the soil's compactness or the plant's genetic weakness. Nevertheless, it is still no big thing to lose a clump of Indian blanketflowers or Shasta daisies.

❧ When it comes to larger plants like shrubs and trees, the gardener's feelings begin to change.

❧ We select and plant a tree with care. We weigh the pros and cons of one tree against the other, symmetry against free form, and from the day we put the tree in the ground—and buying and planting a tree is always a celebration—we watch it with anxiety and anticipation. Is it getting too tall too quickly, or is it spreading too wide? Should it be pruned to develop a central leader, or is it healthier to cut off that incipient trunk and encourage several competing branches around it instead?

❧ The death of a tree is not serene—not even if the tree fell in such a way that it hurt no one and nothing. But we gardeners tend not to rage against the dying of the light. We watch plants go gently into that good night, and usually we are far too busy tidying up and replanting to take time out for mourning.

❧ Death in the garden does not have the finality of clods thudding against a coffin, and when we feel distress at the loss of a much loved tree, we are projecting onto the plant feelings about our own mortality. For plants, what we call death is only the passing from one type of existence to another, and when we think of that, the idea of reincarnation makes solid common sense. After all, every year withered leaves break down in the compost pile, and in this new form, they help make the soil richer and more porous for living plants that sprout and grow and bloom. Dense debris such as chopped-up branches and rotted tree trunks can be first applied as mulch that preserves vital moisture before it finally breaks up and thus enhances the soil.

&❧ It is not morbid to think about wanting to be buried as "fill." My wish for myself is to be laid to rest in a pine box that should disintegrate in ten years. Together, we will enrich the earth.